THE AB GUIDE TO MUSIC THEORY

The AB Guide to Music Theory

Part II

ERIC TAYLOR

The Associated Board of
the Royal Schools of Music

First published in 1991 by
The Associated Board of the Royal Schools of Music (Publishing) Ltd
14 Bedford Square, London WC1B 3JG

© 1991 by The Associated Board of the Royal Schools of Music

ISBN 1 85472 447 9

Typesetting and music processing by
Halstan & Co. Ltd, Amersham, Bucks
Printed in Great Britain by
Dotesios Ltd, Trowbridge

CONTENTS

Chapter 19: String instruments

Chapter 20: Woodwind and Brass instruments

Chapter 21: Percussion and Keyboard instruments

Chapter 22: Instruments in combination

Chapter 23: Before the tonal period

Chapter 24: Some modern developments

ACKNOWLEDGEMENTS

Thanks are due to the following publishers for permission to reproduce passages from copyright music:

Boosey & Hawkes Music Publishers Ltd
    Bartók, Sonata for two pianos and percussion
    Britten, *Prince of the Pagodas*
    Prokofiev, *Classical Symphony*

Editio Musica Budapest
    Bartók, Bagatelle No.1 for piano

Editions Durand S.A./United Music Publishers Ltd
    Messiaen, Piano Prelude No.5
    Messiaen, *Quartet for the end of time*

Faber Music Ltd
    Folksong, 'Edward'

Novello & Co. Ltd
    Brahms, *A German Requiem* (English version)

Stainer & Bell Ltd
    Vaughan Williams, Prelude on the Welsh hymn tune 'Rhosymedre'

Universal Edition (London) Ltd
    Schoenberg, Variations for Orchestra, Op.31

PART II

CHAPTER 14

Voices

Most of the points of notation discussed in Part I of *The AB Guide to Music Theory* are common property to all musicians and are used by singers and instrumentalists alike, but there are others which are applicable only to particular instruments. Usually, in fact, they are technical playing instructions: how a violin passage is to be bowed, for example, or how piano pedals are to be used. Details of this kind can greatly affect the sounds produced – their colour[1], dynamics and articulation – and thus can be crucial to the total musical effect.

Evidently, then, there are essential aspects of musical notation which require even non-players to possess some knowledge of the special characteristics of individual instruments. And there is a further complication: how notation combines the separate parts of a group of musicians performing together simultaneously, as in a choir or orchestra. The special problems of notating music for voices will be considered in this chapter; those which concern instruments will be discussed in Chapters 19–22.

14/1 Singers and choirs

People have voices of different pitch: the voices of women, girls and boys are higher than those of men, for example. Not only that, some women have higher voices than others, and men's voices vary similarly. Most commonly, voices are divided into four groups: **Soprano, Alto, Tenor, Bass**. Their approximate ranges are:

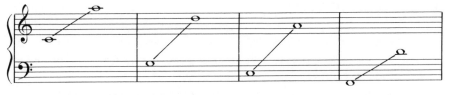

[1]Other words for 'colour' are 'tone quality', 'tone' (not to be confused with the interval) and 'timbre'.

This is only a rough-and-ready guide, however, since people vary considerably not only in their natural voices but also in the extent to which their voices have been developed. Trained singers may manage a few notes above or below those shown, or both; untrained singers may well have a much more limited range.

The division of voices into sopranos, altos, tenors and basses (often abbreviated as 'S A T B') can be somewhat arbitrary: as we shall see later, there are some singers whose voices lie between these categories. Nevertheless, the SATB grouping is the most usual when different voices are combined, especially in choirs and choruses.

Nowadays, both 'choir' and 'chorus' imply a group of singers, with each section – sopranos, altos etc. – being sung by more than one singer. The two words are virtually interchangeable, although a group of singers in church services is usually described as a choir, and one in a stage production (e.g. an opera or a musical) as a chorus.

Tenor and bass parts are always sung by men. The soprano part is sung by women or girls, or by boys with unbroken voices: traditionally, church and cathedral choirs used boys' voices, though they are more often called **trebles** rather than sopranos. In the traditional church or cathedral choir, the alto part is sung by men with high voices (or using a special technique known as *falsetto* singing). Elsewhere, e.g. in opera or oratorio choruses, women's voices are more usual. A *solo* woman singer with an alto range is always called a **contralto**, not an alto; but a *group* of women with the same range may be referred to either as contraltos or altos.

The most common type of choir or chorus is a four-part combination of sopranos (or trebles), altos (or contraltos), tenors and basses. This is the grouping normally used, for example, in church hymns. It is also found in many choral and operatic works such as Purcell's *Dido and Aeneas*, Handel's *Messiah*, Mendelssohn's *Elijah* and Britten's *Peter Grimes*, to name but a few examples at random.

14/2 Voices in score

Often it is practicable to write all four voices on two staves, with the soprano and alto parts on the upper stave in the treble clef and the tenor and bass parts on the lower stave in the bass clef. This is particularly convenient when the voices change notes together, or mostly together, as in hymn tunes and chorales, e.g. –

S. Webbe, *Melcombe*

In a two-stave arrangement the stems of the soprano and tenor notes *always* go up and those of the alto and bass go down, however high or low they may lie on the stave. Thus, if this were written for alto and soprano –  , the soprano would sing A and the alto C. Had those two notes been semibreves, guide-lines would have been needed to show the crossing of parts –

If the parts cross frequently, or if they have much independence of rhythmic movement, it is more satisfactory to write them on separate lines. In this fragment from *A German Requiem* by Brahms[1], for example, the singers would have no difficulty in following their individual parts –

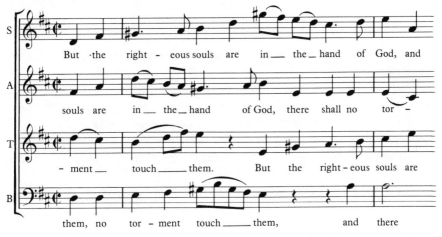

[1] English version adapted from the Bible by Ivor Atkins (copyright Novello & Co. Ltd).

But if the passage is squeezed on to two staves, it becomes very congested and difficult to sort out –

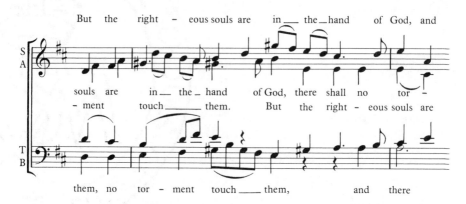

It is important to compare the tenor part in these two versions. In the compressed, two-stave version it is written in the bass clef and at its true pitch; but when it has a stave to itself (as in the four-stave version), the tenor is written not only in the treble clef but also an octave higher than it actually sounds. The reason for the latter notation is that it avoids the necessity for many ledger lines. It is a convention which is well understood: often, as in the passage quoted above, there is no special sign to show that, when tenors sing notes in the treble clef, they are to sing them an octave lower than written. Nevertheless, it is not a good principle to use one sign to mean two different things; and to prevent any possibility of confusion various symbols have sometimes been added to the treble clef to show that the notes are to be sung an octave lower. Thus and and all mean that the note to be sung is actually . The first and second of these signs are now obsolete, but the third – the little 8 below the treble clef – has become standard.

When each voice is written on a separate stave, the music is said to be in **open score**; if compressed into two staves it is in **short score**. (These terms are also applied to instrumental music.) A **vocal score** shows the music of a composition for voices and instruments (usually an orchestra) with the voice parts given in full – in either short or open score – but with the instrumental parts adapted and arranged so that they can be played on the piano[1].

Although choirs and choruses most commonly consist of SATB, other groupings are often found, divided into fewer or more parts. For example,

[1]Other uses of the word 'score' are explained in Chapter 22.

there may be no sopranos (leaving ATB) or no basses (SAT). Further, any of the SATB parts may be divided into two or more separate lines. When this happens, they are described as first and second sopranos ($S_1 S_2$) or first and second basses ($B_1 B_2$) etc. The choir in Bach's great B minor Mass, for instance, is mostly divided into five parts: $S_1 S_2 ATB$ (as in the opening *Kyrie*), but the *Sanctus* uses six ($S_1 S_2 A_1 A_2 TB$) and some sections use only four (SATB). In the *Osanna* the singers are divided into two separate choirs: $S_1 A_1 T_1 B_1$; $S_2 A_2 T_2 B_2$; this arrangement is called a **double choir**. As far back as the 16th century, Thomas Tallis wrote a famous motet, *Spem in alium*, in forty parts: eight five-part choirs. Choirs may also consist of women only, or of men only, such as $S_1 S_2 A$ or $T_1 T_2 B_1 B_2$. Numbers are often omitted in describing choral groupings, e.g. SSATB or TTBB.

As was mentioned earlier, the basic division of choirs into SATB is somewhat arbitrary, since the voices of many singers lie somewhere between these ranges, e.g. not quite as low as a bass but not quite as high as a tenor. A voice of this last category is called a **baritone**. Similarly, a **mezzo-soprano** has a range between that of a soprano and a contralto, and a **basso-profundo** is an exceptionally low bass. **Counter-tenor**, on the other hand is merely another term for a male alto.

CHAPTER 15

Non-harmony notes

Earlier in this book (Part I, p.57), 'harmony' was said to consist of 'mixtures of simultaneous sounds of different pitch'. In more detail, the word is used to refer to the ways in which chords are constructed and to the ways in which individual chords relate to each other. 'Tonal harmony' means the kind of harmony found in music written during the 17th–19th centuries (and much that has been written since), for although music developed greatly during this period, evolving many different forms and styles, it continued to be rooted in certain principles.

The two most fundamental principles were the building of music out of notes forming major and minor scales, and the varying degrees of importance attached to these notes (the tonic, the key-note, being the most important of all). Other basic issues include triads and the chords derived from them, and the use of chords at cadences. These matters were considered in Part I. Chapters 15–17 now go further into the workings of tonal harmony.

The first point to be explained is that the notes heard at any one moment do not always belong to the particular chord being used. Other, 'non-harmony', notes[1] may be added as decorations of the melody, or of any part in the music which has a 'melodic line'. This could be the bass line, or an inner part (such as the alto or tenor in a piece for SATB). Non-harmony notes may be simply ornamental, but they can also be deeply expressive. This chapter deals with the most common types. The non-harmony notes are marked *.

15/1 Passing notes

Passing notes are used to provide a link between two notes in a melodic line. The simplest kind is a single passing note between two harmony notes which are a third apart. The two harmony notes may belong to the same chord, e.g. –

(C major)

[1]They are also known as 'non-harmonic' notes – or as 'unessential' or 'inessential' notes, though the last two terms are misleading since the notes in question may well be essential to the effect of the music.

or to different positions of the same chord –

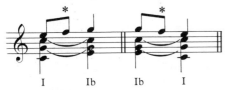

or to different chords –

Notice that in each of these examples, the passing note is dissonant (i.e. it makes a discord[1]) with at least one note in the chord to which it is attached. In the last one, for instance, the E on the top line of the stave makes a discord with the D at the bottom.

Harmony notes which are a major second apart may be linked by a chromatic passing note –

Two or more passing notes may be used in succession to provide the link between two harmony notes –

Passing notes are found not only in the melody but also in the bass and in middle parts –

[1]See Part I, 7/5

They are also used simultaneously in different parts of the music (e.g. in the melody and in the bass or the middle parts) –

Most commonly, passing notes are found in relatively weak positions rhythmically, e.g. as the second of a pair of quavers. All those demonstrated so far are examples. But they also occur in relatively strong positions (usually 'on the beat'), when they are referred to as 'accented passing notes'. Compare, for instance, these two examples –

where the first F is an ordinary (i.e. unaccented) passing note but the second F is an accented passing note. Similarly, compare

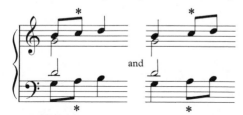

Notice that a passing note always moves from and to a note which is next to it. Other ways of putting this are to say that passing notes move 'by step', or that the movement is 'stepwise' or 'conjunct'.

The following quotations illustrate the use of passing notes –

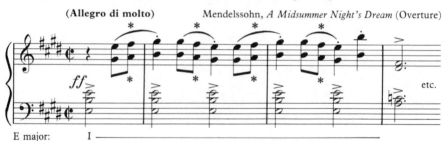

Chopin, Mazurka, Op.7 No.1

J. S. Bach, Chorale 'Machs mit mir'

15/2 Auxiliary notes

An auxiliary note is a note which follows a harmony note by step, either above or below, but then returns to the *same* harmony note. The opening of the well-known song, 'Wiegenlied',[1] provides examples –

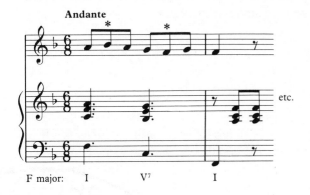

[1] Although it is often attributed to Mozart, it was actually by a contemporary, Bernhard Flies.

Where an auxiliary note would normally lie a whole tone above or below the harmony note, it can be chromatically altered to make the interval a semitone, e.g. –

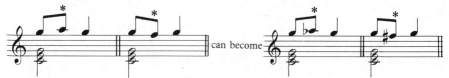

Some of the ornaments described in Chapter 12 (Part I) involve the use of auxiliary notes. The upper and lower mordents use the upper and lower auxiliaries respectively, and the turn uses both (see Part I, p.94).

15/3 Anticipations

These are almost self-explanatory: an anticipation is the sounding of a note *before* the chord to which it belongs. Good examples occur at the opening of the Minuet in Beethoven's Septet, Op.20[1] –

As in this passage, anticipations are generally a step away from the previous harmony note. They are very common at cadences.

15/4 Changing notes

This section will group together a variety of non-harmony notes involving movement both by step and by leap. If only one non-harmony note is used,

---

[1] He also used the same theme (though in G major) in the second movement of the Piano Sonata, Op.49 No.2.

the step may come after the first harmony note, e.g.  or

, or before the second, e.g. . Two stepwise

movements can also be used together, e.g. , to produce

patterns containing two non-harmony notes.

The first of the patterns outlined above represents a decoration known by the French word *échappée* (or by its English equivalent – an 'escape' note). Before the first harmony note goes to the second, the melody moves one step in the opposite direction, e.g. –

(These chords are merely outlines of typical harmonisations: as in the examples which follow, other harmonisations and other lay-outs are possible. Similarly, the given rhythms are only specimens: many others can be devised. Illustrations of the actual application of the underlying principles are given in the quotations of music passages on pp.116–7.)

Apart from the échappée, there is much confusion over the names given to the non-harmony notes in this section. To avoid becoming ensnared in this, it is best to describe them all as **changing notes**.[1] (The échappée is just a particular kind of changing note.)

In other patterns containing a single non-harmony note, the stepwise movement comes before the second harmony note, e.g. –

---

[1]The Italian for 'changing note' is *nota cambiata*, or just *cambiata* by itself. Both of these expressions are often used in English too, but they can cause misunderstanding: 'nota cambiata' is also used in more restricted senses (particularly in 15th- and 16th-century music), while the single word 'cambiata' has been used with both specific and general meanings in reference to later music.

These are typical patterns involving two changing notes together –

Patterns can also be found which do not quite fit into any of the above categories, although they are similar. Usually they can be regarded as slight variations. In both of the following passages, for instance, the first non-harmony note is a changing note followed not by a harmony note but by a passing note –

The following quotations all include examples of changing notes (marked *) –

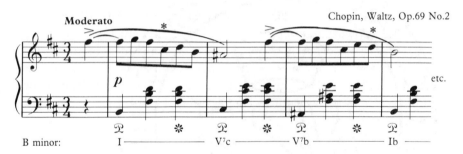

Chopin, Waltz, Op.69 No.2

B minor: I ——————— V⁷c ——————— V⁷b ——————— Ib ——

Rossini, *The Barber of Seville* ('Largo al factotum')

C major: I ——————

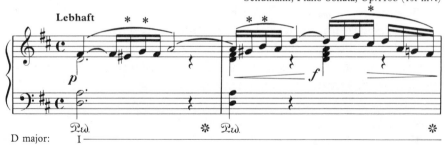

Schumann, Piano Sonata, Op.118b (1st mvt)

D major: I ——————

15/5 Appoggiaturas[1]

Because appoggiaturas used to be written in a special way, there has already been some discussion of them in the chapter about 'Ornaments and Embellishments' (Part I, 12/2c). The special notation described there began to be abandoned in the late 18th century. Nevertheless, composers continued to write appoggiaturas – but using ordinary notation, i.e. in full-size notes and with the correct time values. (Examples of both methods will be found in the quotations below.)

---

[1]Strictly speaking, *appoggiatura* is an Italian word and its plural should therefore be *appoggiature*. However, like 'sonata' and many other Italian words used in music, it has become a standard word in English: hence the 'Englished' plural used here.

The appoggiatura was originally so called because of its melodic shape: it 'leans' on the following note. At first (in the early 17th century) it was thought of chiefly as a *melodic* decoration; but gradually an increasing importance was given to it as a source of *harmonic* enrichment. Both melodic and harmonic features are indispensable to the appoggiatura in the modern meaning of the word. To illustrate these features, here are some typical patterns (with the appoggiaturas marked *) –

I   VI   I   VI

The essential points to note are these:

1) An appoggiatura is a dissonant note: it makes a discord with at least one other note in the chord to which it is attached.

2) An appoggiatura is followed by the note below or above it. This note, the 'resolution', is one of the notes of the same chord.

3) An appoggiatura is placed in a more strongly accented position than its resolution: the musical effect is of a strong note followed by a weak one.

An appoggiatura which is approached by step could also, of course, be described as an accented passing note, e.g. –

II   V   II   VI

Often it is immaterial which it is called. However, the longer and the more accented the dissonant note is, the more appropriate becomes the term 'appoggiatura'. And when written in the old way (as a small-size note), it is always an appoggiatura – no matter how short it may be.

The following quotations are not merely examples of the technical aspects of the appoggiatura: they also show that it can be a powerful means of expression, particularly in setting words to music. The effect is heightened when two or more are used simultaneously (as in the Elgar example, which is for large chorus and orchestra).

Mozart, Violin Sonata, K.547 (3rd mvt)

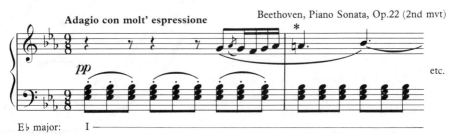

F major: I   VIIb   V⁷b   I

Adagio con molt' espressione   Beethoven, Piano Sonata, Op.22 (2nd mvt)

Eb major: I

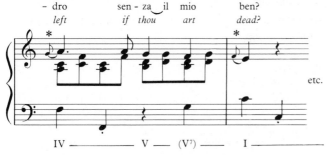

C major: I   V⁷   Ib

IV ———————— V —— (V⁷) —— I ————

---

[1] As well as the original Italian words, a familiar English translation (by Claude Aveling) is given. Although the English version is not exact, it contrives to make important words coincide with the musical accents – especially at the appoggiaturas. The Italian includes some elisions (see Part I, p.42).

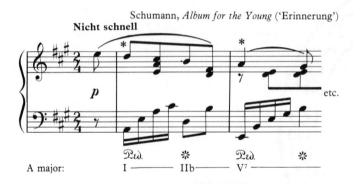

15/6 Suspensions

A harmony note may be delayed in moving to the next chord: it is left behind for a moment when the other notes of the chord change. If at this point it becomes dissonant with the new chord, it is called a **suspension**. Compare, for example, these two progressions –

They are identical, except that in the second example one note has been delayed. What happens is that the C in the melody is held up, and is late in moving to the following note (B). In other words, the C has been 'suspended'.

Thus there are three notes involved in the suspension process. Each has a technical name:

1) the **preparation**, which is always a harmony note;
2) the **suspension** itself, which is a continuation of the same note; and
3) the **resolution**, which again is always a harmony note.

Here the three notes have been ringed –

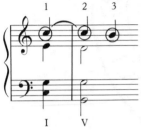

The suspended note produces a discord. (In the example above, the C after the bar-line is dissonant with the D below it, and also with the Gs in the bass clef.) Consequently, although the next passage looks rather similar, the note marked + is *not* a suspension since it is a harmony note and not a discord –

(The only non-harmony note here is the B, which is a passing note.)

Two other important details to notice are:

a) The resolution is always a note below or a note above the suspension. In the examples given so far it was always a note below, which is the more common. Suspensions which resolve upwards are sometimes called 'retardations', e.g. –

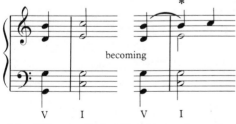

b) The resolution is always in a rhythmically weaker position than the suspended note: typically the suspension occurs on a strong beat and the resolution on the following weak beat.

Suspensions are often used in the bass, and in the middle of the music. e.g. –

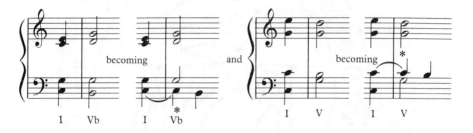

Two or even three suspensions may be used simultaneously, e.g. –

From a purely harmonic point of view, a suspension is virtually identical with one type of appoggiatura: an appoggiatura preceded by the same note. Compare, for instance,

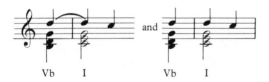

The only difference between the two examples is the lack of a tie in the second. Nevertheless, because the D is repeated and not tied in the second example, it is strictly an appoggiatura, not a suspension.

For the sake of clarity, all the suspensions illustrated above have been shown as notes tied over a bar-line. Suspensions used in the middle of a bar may be less obvious when they are notated without ties, e.g. –

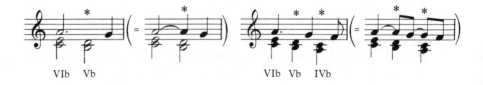

One other point remains to be made. Between the suspension and its resolution, another note – or other notes – may be inserted. Usually these added notes are other notes belonging to the chord (e.g. 1 and 2 below), or changing notes (e.g. 3), or mixtures of these (e.g. 4) – possibly linked by passing notes (e.g. 5).

In the following quotations the suspensions are marked * –

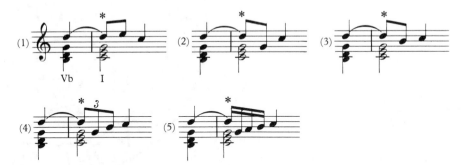

D. Scarlatti, The 'Cat' Fugue

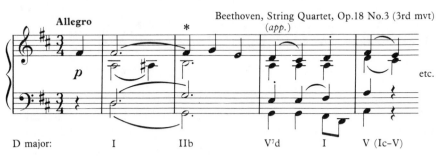

Beethoven, String Quartet, Op.18 No.3 (3rd mvt)
(app.)

J. S. Bach, Invention No.13

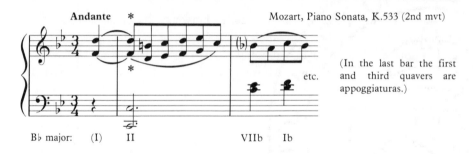

(In the last bar the first and third quavers are appoggiaturas.)

15/7 Pedal points

A **pedal point**, generally known simply as a 'pedal', is a note which is sustained throughout changing harmonies. This sustained note need not 'belong' to each of the chords which it accompanies, and is often dissonant with them. Most commonly, it is found in the bass. Indeed, in organ music it can actually *be* a pedal note: the organist keeps his foot on a low note on the pedal board while playing independent music on the manuals. (The opening of both of Bach's C minor Fantasias for the organ provide examples.) But the device is not confined to the organ. Here is an example for piano: from Debussy's Prelude, *La Cathédrale engloutie* –

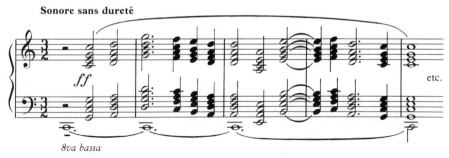

In this particular passage, of course, the harmonies used over the pedal are just an uninterrupted succession of second-inversion chords: a progression which was an innovation in the early 20th century (see p.243). The chords used in earlier times followed earlier harmonic conventions, but still went their way as though the bass were not there. Thus the opening of Beethoven's Piano Sonata in E (Op.14 No.1), for instance, consists essentially of these chords –

over the pedal note E in the bass:

Notice here that the bass is not literally sustained – i.e. it is not a string of tied semibreves; nevertheless the persistence of the E gives the effect of a sustained note.

Pedal points may last for only two or three changes of chord, or they can be much longer. Also, they are not necessarily restricted to the bass: they can be used at the top of the music or, as here, in the middle, e.g. –

Schumann, *Album for the Young* ('Trällerliedchen')

This is no more than an elaboration of –

A pedal point at the top of the music may be called an 'inverted pedal', and one in the middle of the texture an 'inner pedal'.

CHAPTER 16

More about tonal harmony

16/1 Counterpoint

As was seen in Chapter 14, a piece written for a choir consists of a combination of individual parts: e.g. SATB. Consequently, there must always be a note (or a rest) for each of the parts – even when they are written in short score as in the Brahms quotations on pp.107–8 (but see the footnote on p.164).

When all the parts keep together[1] – as in many hymn tunes – the individual parts are not always very tuneful. Normally the top line is a genuine melody, and to some extent the bass also will have a feeling of melodic shaping, but the inner parts are often rather dull. The alto part in the following is a case in point –

W. H. Monk, Hymn tune 'Eventide'

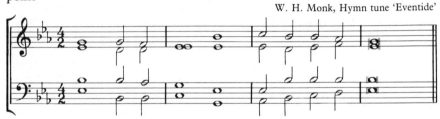

Often, however, the parts are designed to have an *equal* melodic interest, with independent rhythms. When this happens, the music is described as **counterpoint**, or it is said to be 'contrapuntal'. Again, the passage by Brahms referred to above provides an example.

Naturally, contrapuntal music can be performed not only by groups of voices but also by groups of instruments, such as a string quartet. It can be performed, too, by solo keyboard instruments, and frequently is (although piano music in particular more often uses other textures, such as arpeggiated and broken-chord patterns: see Part I, 8/5). Many pieces for keyboard include some passages which are contrapuntal and some which are not. Examples of keyboard works which are contrapuntal throughout are the two-part Inventions and the three-part Sinfonias of J. S. Bach.

A characteristic of these two collections is that in each of the pieces the individual parts are based on the same melodic ideas, e.g. –

[1]This chordal style is known as 'homophony' (from Greek words meaning 'same sound'). Music written in this style is 'homophonic'. The terms 'polyphony' ('several sounds') and 'polyphonic' are sometimes used simply as alternatives for 'counterpoint' and 'contrapuntal'; but generally they are reserved for unaccompanied choral music, particularly from the 16th and earlier centuries.

J. S. Bach, Invention No.7

Counterpoint of this kind is described as 'imitative'. It is an essential feature of the form of composition known as **fugue** (see p.189): notable examples are those in Bach's 48 Preludes and Fugues. The most exact kind of imitative counterpoint is **canon**: two (or more) parts are the same, but starting one after another, e.g. –

(Variations of this basic principle are also used, as when the second part transposes the first, e.g. a perfect 5th higher). If, when it gets to the end, each part starts again from the beginning, the canon is said to be 'perpetual'. And a perpetual canon for voices, in which *all* the voices sing the same melody at the same pitch, is a **round**. 'Three blind mice' and 'London's burning' are well-known traditional rounds.

Not all counterpoint is imitative, however. A famous passage towards the end of Wagner's Prelude to *The Mastersingers*, for instance, combines three quite distinct melodies which have been heard separately earlier. But whether imitative or not, music which is contrapuntal always has a harmonic basis as well. The individual parts combine to produce chords – or, at the very least, to *imply* chords very clearly. (Sometimes not all the notes of a chord are actually present.) The chord basis of the opening of the Bach Invention quoted on p.127, for instance, can be represented thus –

E minor: I   V   I

Each and every note in the counterpoint is either a harmony note or a non-harmony note related to a harmony note (in one of the ways described in Chapter 15). Below is the same passage again, with the non-harmony notes marked. Three types are used: passing notes (marked '*p*'), auxiliary notes (marked '*a*'), and an échappée (marked '*e*').

The individual contrapuntal lines may be described as the 'horizontal' aspect of the music (on paper they are written *along* the staves ⟶), and the chords which they form as the 'vertical' aspect of the music (on paper they are written *down* the staves ↓).

16/2 Part-writing

When two voices or instrumental parts move from one note to the next keeping the same interval between them, they are said to move 'in parallel motion', e.g. –

Parallel motion tends to undermine counterpoint, because the more two melodic lines move together in this way the less they can be said to be independent of each other.

In practice, it would be quite impossible for parallel motion to be avoided altogether in contrapuntal music. Nevertheless, as long ago as the 15th century certain progressions seem to have been regarded as particularly damaging to the effect of independent parts, and it became the convention to avoid using consecutive unisons, consecutive perfect octaves, and consecutive perfect 5ths. Also avoided were the compounds of these intervals, e.g. consecutive perfect 12ths and 15ths. By these standards, all the following examples are to be considered faulty, because of the 'forbidden' consecutive intervals marked with square brackets –

These conventions lasted until the late 19th century, but with some variations of detail at different periods. J. S. Bach, for instance, occasionally wrote consecutive perfect 5ths in his chorales when they resulted from the use of a non-harmony note. An example occurs in the chorale, 'Bin ich gleich von dir gewichen', from the *St Matthew Passion*, where the quaver A in the soprano is an anticipation –

Attitudes have varied, too, to consecutive 5ths and octaves produced by 'contrary motion', e.g. –

At first, these were used only in certain circumstances, and never when they occurred between the top and the bottom voices or instruments. By the classical period, however, composers had become more relaxed about them; and even between outer parts contrary-motion octaves (though not 5ths) became a commonplace at perfect cadences, e.g. –

Mozart, Piano Sonata, K.331 (1st mvt)

Conventions about the avoidance of consecutive 5ths and octaves come under the general heading of what is called **part-writing** (or, particularly in the U.S.A., 'voice-leading'). 'Part-writing' refers to the ways in which contrapuntal parts are related to each other, and also to the ways in which they are individually shaped to produce good melodic lines. Thus some technical details which were considered earlier also come under this heading. Examples include the ways in which dissonant intervals contained in chords (notably the 7th in a V⁷ chord) are resolved, and the ways in which suspensions are used.

Part-writing in contrapuntal music written for keyboard (as in the Bach Inventions, Sinfonias etc.) is not essentially any different from part-writing written for a combination of voices or instruments. When keyboard music is clearly not contrapuntal, the ordinary conventions about part-writing do not apply (as in the left-hand chords in the Mozart example opposite). Nevertheless, virtually all tonal music – keyboard music included – has *some* contrapuntal aspects. In this respect, the bass is particularly important. Usually it has real melodic shape, even though it may be much simpler then anything which may be going on above it, e.g. –

Schubert, Impromptu, D.899/4

or may only be outlined, e.g. –

Brahms, Waltz, Op.39 No.9

Here the implied bass, with chord indications, is –

D minor: I   VII⁷b   Ib   IV

Consequently, the bass will make two-part counterpoint with any melody or melodic fragment above it (e.g. the melody in the upper part of the bass stave in the Schubert example). The two together will then follow the ordinary conventions of part-writing.

Before leaving the subject of part-writing, it should be mentioned that the convention of avoiding consecutive octaves does not extend to a whole passage performed in octaves: e.g. a melody 'doubled' an octave higher, or a bass doubled an octave lower. Such passages do not constitute two separate melodic lines: merely one which has been reinforced.

16/3 Harmonic rhythm

The rate at which the basic harmonies of a piece change is generally considerably slower than the rate of the actual notes heard. For example, the opening of Mendelssohn's 'Italian' Symphony gives an impression of great activity and vitality, with rapidly moving notes, yet its underlying harmonies are changing with much less haste –

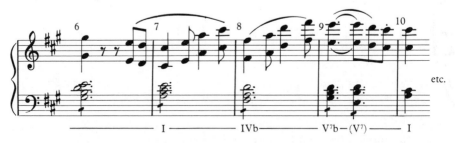

Here, there is only one chord (I) in bars 1–4, and one (V) in bars 5–6. The chords change more frequently in bars 7–10, but even these bars have only one harmony each (bar 9 being dominant throughout). This pattern of chord-changes forms a rhythm of its own: the **harmonic rhythm** of the passage. It could be represented thus –

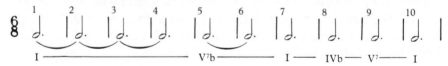

Usually, harmonic rhythm is not only slower but also simpler than any of the rhythms which are in fact being played. Nevertheless, it is of the greatest importance in the shaping of music: *when* chords change is as important as *which* chords are used. This can easily be demonstrated by changing the chords at different places in bars 3–7 of the Mendelssohn example quoted above –

The altered version produces an unbalanced harmonic rhythm –

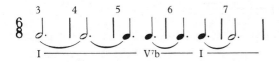

and in doing so wrecks the entire balance of the phrase. The harmonic rhythm no longer reinforces the natural rhythm of the melody, in which a regular pattern of alternating strong and weak beats is created by the relatively long notes at the beginning of each bar. (Further emphasis is given by the pitches used, with the highest and lowest notes occurring on strong beats.)

Another common feature is illustrated by the quotation from the 'Italian' Symphony: the harmonic rhythm quickens (the chords change more frequently) as it approaches the cadence in bars 9–10. Consequently the music becomes more intense before it relaxes at the cadence. In this way the harmonic rhythm helps to shape the phrase.

16/4 Second-inversion chords

Non-harmony notes do not destroy the effect of the basic chords in a piece or of the underlying harmonic rhythm which they produce. Consider, for instance, the following progression (a) from a tonic to a dominant chord, both in root position. It does not cease to be felt as such when it moves via an inversion (b), or when it is further decorated with various passing and auxiliary notes (c–e).

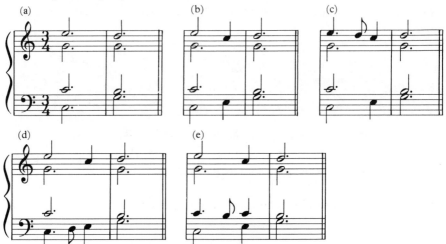

What may seem to be a different situation arises if all these non-harmony notes are combined, for then what appears to be an extra chord is produced: a Vc (at +) –

But this combination of notes is not so much a chord in its own right as a by-product. It is not really an independent chord at all: it has only a subsidiary status.

A pair of auxiliary notes can produce a similar situation –

Again, the combination of notes at + does not constitute a separate and different chord, as can be illustrated by the opening of Brahms' Variations on a theme of Haydn –

In this passage, the first bar is clearly heard as one chord (I_____), not three (I–IVc–I). Consequently the harmonic rhythm is ♪ ♩ | ♩ ♩ |, not ♪ ♩.♩♩ | ♩ ♩ |.

Although other subsidiary chords can be produced by combinations of non-harmony notes, so called 'second-inversion' ($^6_4$) chords are the most common. Indeed, they originated as the product of a double suspension, e.g. –

and up to about the end of the 16th century were only used in this form. Later, they also resulted from the use of a pair of appoggiaturas, e.g. –

In both cases the true harmonic rhythm is ♩ | ♩ (not ♩♩ ♩).

$^6_4$ chords produced by double appoggiaturas are a commonplace in music of the classical period, particularly at cadences. An example by Beethoven was quoted earlier (the last two beats of the extract on p.123), and one by Haydn was included in Part I (p.74).

It would be an exaggeration, however, to assert that *all* $^6_4$ chords are mere adjuncts of other chords. The first chord in the Elgar example on p.120, for instance, is not, since it is far too weighty and extended to be felt as anything but an essential chord in its own right.

16/5 Extensions of the triad (7ths, 9ths etc.)

As was illustrated on p.61 (Part I), a triad on any degree of the scale may be extended by the addition of a 7th from the root. The most common occurrence of this – a 7th added to the dominant triad, forming the dominant 7th chord – was considered in 8/2 and 9/2b. The 7th chords on other degrees of the scale are collectively known as 'secondary sevenths'. Like the dominant 7th, they take their individual names from the degrees of the scale on which they are based: e.g. a 7th chord on the 2nd degree of the scale (II⁷) is a 'supertonic 7th'.

In all 7th chords, the 7th itself is resolved in the following chord, normally by moving one step down or, very occasionally, by staying where it is, e.g. –

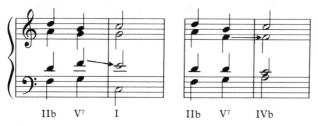

    IIb   V⁷   I   IIb   V⁷   IVb

The only standard exception to this is when the second inversion of a V⁷ occurs between I and Ib, and the 7th rises one step e.g. –

    I   V⁷c   Ib

The V⁷c in this progression, however, is another 'second-inversion' chord produced by non-harmony notes: the F in the melody (like the D in the bass) is heard simply as a passing note, with the B as an auxiliary note. (It is worth noticing that the parallel 5ths which arise in the last two chords – top stave – do not break the convention regarding consecutive 5ths mentioned in 16/2 since they are not both *perfect* 5ths: B–F is a diminished 5th.)

What is popularly known as the **added sixth** chord is sometimes regarded as a type of secondary 7th chord. Originally, however, the term was used to describe a subdominant chord to which a 6th from the root had been added as a passing note –

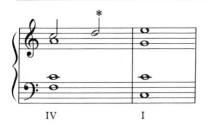

IV   I

Here, the combination of notes produced by the passing note (*) is clearly another by-product rather than a chord in its own right. In different circumstances, however, the same notes can form what is a truly independent chord –

VI   II⁷b   V

Nowadays, this II⁷b chord would also be described as an 'added sixth', as indeed would any chord consisting of a major or minor triad plus a 6th from the root. One such chord became a cliché in jazz and popular music: a 6th added to a final tonic chord. In this situation it would of course be absurd to label the chord as VI⁷b, e.g. in C major –

Further extensions to the basic triad may be made by the addition of a 9th, 11th or 13th from the root, e.g. –

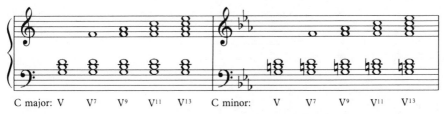

C major: V   V⁷   V⁹   V¹¹   V¹³   C minor: V   V⁷   V⁹   V¹¹   V¹³

However, it is not always possible for all the notes of these chords to be

included. Even 7th chords may lack a 3rd or 5th, e.g.

This may be because of the demands of good part-writing, or simply because all four notes *cannot* be performed – e.g. in a piece for three solo voices. Similarly, there are too many notes in 9th, 11th, and 13th chords for them all to be included in a piece written for SATB or in one written in four-part counterpoint. But even where complete chords are possible (e.g. in keyboard music) notes are frequently omitted. The 5th from the root is the most likely note to be missing, as in the V^9 chord in the third bar of this passage (at +) –

In the next example the 5th, 9th and 11th from the root are not included in the V^{13} (at +) –

It is interesting to compare this cadence by Grieg with one by Schubert –

The chord marked + could be explained as IIIb in G. Nevertheless, it has a strong dominant character, producing the effect of a perfect cadence, and for this reason might be regarded as a V^{13} chord, in spite of the absence of so many notes. There are times in the study of harmony when it can be salutary to remember Shakespeare's lines in *Romeo and Juliet* -

What's in a name? that which we call a rose
By any other name would smell as sweet.

Very often, what may appear to be 9th, 11th and 13th chords are really nothing more than the result of adding appoggiaturas or other non-harmony notes to simpler versions of the same chord. Thus the descriptions of chords contained in square brackets below the following examples are misleading: these chords are merely dominant 7th chords embellished by non-harmony notes (marked *) –

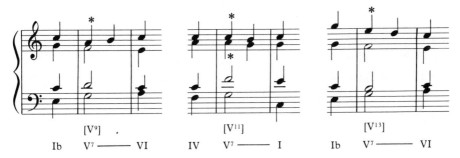

Even harmonic progressions which include 'true' 9th, 11th or 13th chords often closely resemble simpler progressions decorated with non-harmony notes. Compare, for instance, (a) and (b) in each of the following pairs of examples –

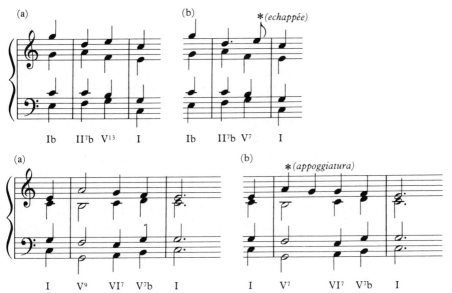

Thus it can often be a fine point whether to describe a chord as a V^7 or as a more extended V chord. The chord marked + in the Grieg quotation on p.138, for instance, is virtually identical (apart from the difference of key) with the chord marked + in this quotation from Mendelssohn –

Mendelssohn, Song without Words, Op.30 No.3

But although the V chord in the Grieg can only be a V^{13}, the V chord in the Mendelssohn could be regarded either as a V^{13} or as a V^7 (with the C$\sharp$ and the G$\sharp$ in the melody as appoggiaturas): i.e. as an elaboration of –

16/6 Modulation

Pieces very rarely stay in the same key throughout. Almost without exception there will be a digression to at least one other key – for the sake of variety and as a means of giving shape to the piece as a whole.

Since the music ultimately returns to the original key, no change of key which occurs during a piece is truly permanent. Nevertheless, an important distinction has to be made between a brief visit to another key and one which is longer-lasting. When the listener feels that the music has really settled in a key, at least for the time being, the key is said to have been 'established'.

A digression to another key is usually described as a **modulation**, but the word is used with different shades of meaning, and this can cause misunderstanding. It is better to think of modulation as a *process* by which one key may lead to another. The most common process involves the use of a 'pivot' chord. A pivot chord is one which can be found both in the first key and in the second: the chord of G major, for instance, can be found both in C major (as V) and in G major (as I). In the following passage, the first chord in bar 3 is approached in C major but left in G major. At the moment when the music arrives at this chord there is no reason to suppose that it is anything other than V in C, but by the time the passage has ended the listener realises that it also functioned as I in G.

The pivot chord here is both V in C major and I in G major.

Two keys may have more than one chord in common: consequently there may be not just one pivot chord but several, e.g. –

The more chords two keys have in common, the more closely they are 'related'.

Instead of a complete chord, one or two notes may act as a pivot. A note of a chord in the first key becomes a note of a different chord in the second key; or the two chords may have two notes in common. In the following examples, the common notes are linked by dotted lines –

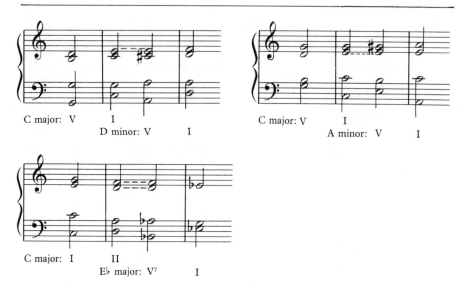

Three quotations will illustrate these modulation processes. The first, from the first movement of Mozart's Piano Sonata, K.457, uses a single pivot chord –

The second quotation is from Elgar's 'Enigma' Variations for orchestra. It starts at the close of Variation 8 (in G major), which ends on the tonic chord. Finally, just the tonic note (G) is left by itself. In a magical moment, the G is then tied over to become the 3rd of a tonic chord in E♭ major at the opening of the 'Nimrod' variation –

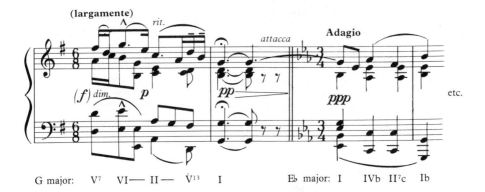

G major: V⁷   VI—— II—— V̇¹³   I   E♭ major: I   IVb II⁷c   Ib

In the third quotation (from the first movement of Beethoven's Piano Sonata, Op.7), two notes provide the connection between the keys of D minor and E♭ major. D and F appear both in the tonic chord of D minor (bars 3–4 of the passage quoted) and in the following chord (bars 5–6), which is the dominant of E♭ major –

D minor: I ——————————— Vc—— (Vb) ——— I ———————————

E♭ major: Vb——— (V⁷b) ——————— I ———————————

The presence of a modulatory process leading towards a new key is no guarantee that the new key will be felt to be established – not even if there is a perfect cadence in the new key. To illustrate this, here are the first four bars of Schumann's 'Merry Peasant' (from *Album for the Young*) –

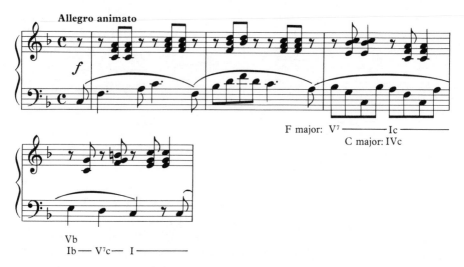

F major: V⁷ ——————— Ic ——————
                C major: IVc

Vb
Ib — V⁷c— I ————————

The passage starts in F major, and modulates to C major by means of pivot chords. But although the last two chords are those which form a perfect cadence (V⁷c–I) in C major, there is no feeling that the music has now *settled* in the key of C major. The original key – F major – is still very much in the listener's mind; and in spite of the modulation, the C major chord at the end is heard as a dominant (in F major) rather than as a tonic (in C major). This can easily be tested by playing a chord of F major after the four bars quoted above.

To give a genuine impression that the original tonic has been superseded by another usually takes a relatively long time. That is why a real key-change is rarely found in short pieces. For the same reason, it cannot be illustrated by a brief quotation. Its effect can easily be appreciated, however, by anyone who takes the trouble to compare the impression given by the C major chord at the end of the Schumann extract quoted above with the impression given by the C major chord which occurs before the first double bar in the first movement of any of Mozart's three Piano Sonatas in F major, or of Beethoven's Piano Sonata, Op.10 No.2. (In each case, the music has settled in C major well before the double bar, but, to ensure a valid comparison, the whole of the music up to the C major chord should be played.)

Finally in this section, it has to be added that music can modulate *through* keys without settling in any of them – even temporarily. This aspect of the matter, however, will have to be deferred to the next chapter (see pp.169–70).

CHAPTER 17

Chromatic chords

A chromatic chord is a chord including at least one note which does not belong to the diatonic scale of the key. (In a minor key, the notes of both the harmonic and the melodic forms of the scale are diatonic.) Chromatic chords may be used in the process of modulation, or they may be used without any hint of modulation – simply for their expressive effect.

17/1 Borrowed chords

Music in a major key may use chords 'borrowed' from the minor key with the same key-note: e.g. a piece in C major may borrow chords from C minor. The chords most commonly borrowed in this way are the diminished chord on II, the minor chord on IV, and the major chord on the flattened VI ($\flat$VI)[1] –

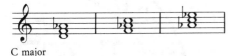

C major

The quotations which follow illustrate each of these possibilities in turn. The first one, the opening of Schumann's song 'Ich grolle nicht' (from *Dichterliebe*), includes the diminished supertonic chord (at *), to which a minor 7th has been added –

Nicht zu schnell
mf

Ich grol-le nicht,   und wenn das   Herz _____ auch bricht,
I'll not com-plain,   e'en though my   heart _____ doth break,

mf etc.

*

[1] A $\flat$ or $\sharp$ sign before a chord indication in roman numerals shows that the root of the chord is lowered or raised a semitone. (See Appendix D.)

The second quotation is the opening of Mendelssohn's Overture to *A Midsummer Night's Dream*. The key is E major, but the third chord (*) is the *minor* subdominant chord –

The third quotation is from the Scherzo of Schubert's Piano Sonata, D.845. The key of the particular passage printed here is C major. The dramatic A♭ chord (*) is the major chord on the ♭VI –

Another example of the ♭VI chord – one used with touching effect – is played by strings at the opening of the last movement of Mahler's 9th Symphony. The key is D♭ major, so the ♭VI is B♭♭. Here (*), however, the composer has written it as A♮ (presumably to make it easier for the cello and double bass players to read) –

An illuminating comparison can be made between this passage and the hymn tune quoted on p.126 since their harmonies are almost identical, except that in the hymn tune the VI is *not* flattened. To make the comparison easier, the Mahler quotation is here transposed into the key of the hymn tune (E♭), and with the true ♭VI in the bass –

It is much rarer for music in minor keys to use chords which have to be regarded as borrowings from the major. This is simply because minor keys themselves already provide many alternatives. They arise out of the fact that the 6th and 7th degrees are variable in the harmonic and melodic forms of the minor scale (see Part I, p.58). In C minor, for example, all of these triads, and the chords derived from them, are strictly diatonic –

However, pieces in minor keys sometimes end with a *major* tonic chord. In this situation the major third itself is known as a *tierce de Picardie* (French for 'Picardy third'). The minor-key pieces in Bach's '48' provide many examples: one of the best known is the ending of the C minor fugue in Book I. It comes at the end of a tonic pedal –

A chromatic chord can act as a pivot chord in a modulation between two keys: a chord which is chromatic in the first key may be diatonic in the second, or vice versa; or it may be chromatic in both keys. Borrowed chords are often used in this way – the next two quotations provide examples. The first is from the first movement of Beethoven's Piano Sonata, Op.10 No.2 –

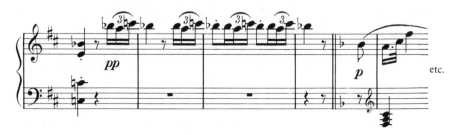

The G minor chord in bar 4 acts as a pivot between D major and F major: it is a minor subdominant chord in the first key and a straightforward supertonic chord (II) in the second.

The second quotation is from the first movement of *A German Requiem* by Brahms –

This passage is played by the orchestra, but the tenors and basses of the chorus enter in the third bar (singing the notes with upward stems in the bass stave). The Db chord here is approached as a chromatic chord in the first key (bVI in F major), but then re-interpreted as the tonic of Db major. (It is in fact the opening of a lengthy section in Db: some editions even insert a double bar and a change of key signature at this point.) The last note at the top of the treble stave (F) also acts as a melodic pivot: it serves both as the tonic in F and as the mediant of Db – a condensed version of the process employed by Elgar in the quotation on p.143.

17/2 Altered chords

Diatonic chords may be changed (e.g. from minor to major) by means of accidentals. When the accidentals produce notes which are chromatic, the chords themselves become chromatic. In C major, for example, –

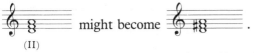

(II)

As well as the notes of the basic triads, diatonic 7ths are sometimes altered so as to produce chromatic 7ths, e.g. –

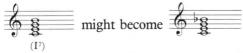

(I⁷)

    The chromatic notes often arise as the result of stepwise movement: i.e. they are often approached and/or left by step. Typical examples occur in No.30 of Schumann's *Album for the Young* –

F major

Here, the gradual ascent of the bass is an important feature (see pp.192–4). Two stages in this ascent are produced by chromatic notes: B♮ and C♯. Both change diatonic chords into chromatic chords. The B♮ changes a II⁷b chord into the first inversion of a chromatic supertonic 7th chord; and the C♯ changes an ordinary Ic into the second inversion of an augmented tonic chord.

    A comparison of the next two quotations, both from Dvořák, illustrates the difference between a chromatically altered note which is approached by step and one which is not. The chromatic note in both cases is the result of sharpening the 5th of a major chord, thus making it augmented (the two chords marked *). In the first passage, the sharpened 5th of the tonic chord (the A♮) can be thought of as a passing note – though a long one. In the second passage, the sharpened 5th of the dominant chord (the A♯) follows a leap (from C).

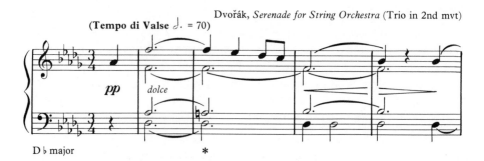

D♭ major   *

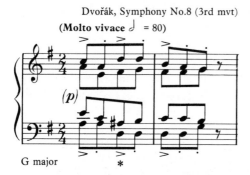

G major   *

When the addition of a chromatic note produces a major chord, the major chord often functions like a V chord in an ordinary V–I progression. Consider, for example, these two progressions in C major –

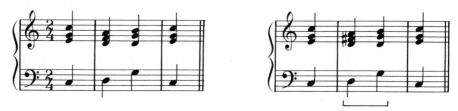

They are of course identical except that, in the second, one note has been altered: the F in the second (supertonic) chord has been changed to F♯. What was a minor chord, therefore, becomes major. This major chord now resembles a dominant: the two chords marked ⌐___⌐ would be V–I if the key were G major. The altered chord could be similarly used in the minor (C minor) –

Chords which function like dominants in this way are known collectively as **secondary dominants**. They may be found on other degrees of the scale apart from the supertonic, as can be seen in the three pairs of examples below. In (a), a ♯ added to the 3rd of a mediant chord (III) in C major transforms it into a secondary dominant leading to VI. At (b), a ♯ added to the 3rd of VI transforms it into a secondary dominant leading to II. And in (c), a ♭ added to the 7th of I⁷b transforms it into a secondary dominant leading to IV.

Playing these examples will show that a secondary dominant does not necessarily create any feeling of modulation. Indeed, it may do the exact opposite: it may strengthen the sense of the tonic key. This happens, for example, in the common cadential progression II–V–I when II is changed into a major chord, thus becoming a secondary dominant to the true dominant. Bach sometimes uses this approach to a perfect cadence in his chorales, where it gives a magnificent feeling of solidity and finality. Two features are usually included which heighten the effect: the chromatic note is made particularly prominent by being placed in the bass (i.e. the chord is used in its first inversion), and the chord is extended to include a 7th. The following quotation (the end of the harmonisation of the chorale melody 'Wir Christenleut' in Cantata No.40) is typical of his use of this chord.

G minor

One other characteristic detail should be noted here: Bach quickly counteracts
the effect of the C♯ in the bass by introducing a C♮ (in the tenor) as a passing
note. This was his usual practice. Composers of the classical and romantic
periods most commonly produced the same result by moving directly to a V
chord *including* the seventh (i.e. a V⁷ chord).

Not surprisingly, altered chords are a very common means of modulation.
The tenor solo, 'Comfort ye my people', in Handel's *Messiah* provides two
examples[1] –

The passage quoted here begins on V of E major, which moves to Ib after the
first bar-line. When the D♮ is added to this chord, the chord becomes
chromatic in E major. But it can now act as a pivot chord – it is also a
straightforward V⁷b in A major, and in fact it resolves on to an A major chord
in the next bar. The root of this chord (A) is then altered to A♯ in the following

[1] The quaver chords of the orchestral accompaniment have been slightly rearranged in order to
fit the music on to two staves, but the harmonies and the bass are not affected.

bar, changing what would otherwise have been a minor chord (VIb in A) into a major chord. This now acts as a dominant to the B major chord in bar 4; and there the music settles for the time being. Notice the bass moving upwards in semitones in this progression: G♯-A-A♯-B. (Further reference to this series of chords will be made on p.169 in discussing harmonic sequences.)

17/3 The Neapolitan sixth

The **Neapolitan sixth** chord probably owes its name to its popularity with composers in Naples during the 17th–18th centuries. It is the first inversion of a major chord on the flattened supertonic (♭IIb): e.g. in C major and C minor –

Although it can be found both in major and in minor keys, it is more common in the latter, and in this context it can be readily understood as another altered chord. Compare, for instance, the following –

I   IIb   V   I   I   ♭IIb(N6) V   I

The use of the Neapolitan 6th chord is illustrated in these quotations –

Beethoven, Piano Sonata, Op.31 No.2 (1st mvt)

(Allegro)

D minor: ♭IIb———   ♭IIb———

A minor: I ——————— ♭IIb ——————— V⁷ ——————— VI ———————

The flattened supertonic chord is less often used in root position. This
example is in C minor –

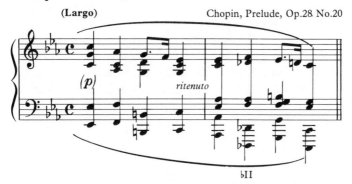

Both in root position and as a Neapolitan 6th, however, the flattened
supertonic chord is the most common means of modulating down a semitone.
Here is a typical example, with the tonic chord of the first key becoming the
♭II of the second –

17/4 The diminished seventh

The structure of the **diminished seventh** chord is easily remembered: it consists of three minor 3rds on top of each other, e.g.  . The chord is named after its most striking interval, the diminished 7th between the top and bottom notes, e.g. – .

Apart from the diminished 7th interval itself, the chord contains two other dissonant intervals: two diminished 5ths – . Each of these dissonances, of course, seeks a resolution, e.g. –

The chord as a whole is most satisfyingly resolved, therefore, when the next chord resolves all the individual dissonances, e.g. , though, as will be seen, it can be followed in other ways.

There is only one circumstance in which a chord consisting of three minor 3rds is a diatonic chord. This is when it occurs as a 7th chord on the leading note of a minor key (VII⁷, e.g. in C minor –), as in this harmonisation of a chorale melody in Bach's *St John Passion* –

G minor: VII⁷

A diminished 7th chord can also be used on the leading note in major keys, and indeed on many other notes in both major and minor keys. In all these situations, however, it is a chromatic chord. For example, the diminished 7th chord on the leading note of C major is chromatic (because of the A♭) –

When it is based on a leading note, the diminished 7th has three notes in common with the first inversion of the dominant 7th, e.g. in C minor –

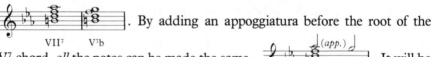 . By adding an appoggiatura before the root of the

V⁷ chord, *all* the notes can be made the same –  It will be

noticed, also, that both chords tend to resolve on to the tonic chord –

These similarities[1] are helpful in understanding how diminished 7th chords operate, for they can function like secondary dominants (without necessarily implying a modulation). Compare, for example, these first inversions of secondary dominants in C major with the diminished 7ths below them –

The following quotations illustrate uses of diminished 7th chords (marked *) which do not lead to a change of key –

Schumann, *Kinderscenen*, ('Wichtige Begebenheit')

[1]Some theorists regard them as more than similarities: in their view the diminished 7th chord *is* a dominant chord – a dominant minor 9th 'with the root missing'. It can often be convenient to think of diminished 7ths in this way, but the explanation does not seem appropriate in all situations.

C minor: *   V   (I)

C major: *   Ic ——————— V

G major: * VIb   * IIb

One characteristic of the diminished 7th chord has far-reaching consequences: when the inversions are spelt differently (changed enharmonically), they continue to consist of three minor 3rds on top of each other, e.g.

In other words, the inversions are enharmonic equivalents of *different* diminished 7th chords: e.g. the three bracketed chords are diminished 7ths on the leading notes of E♭, F♯ and A (major or minor) –

Another way of showing this is to treat each of the notes of a diminished 7th chord in turn as an appoggiatura resolving down a semitone. For example, if the necessary enharmonic changes are made, what was a diminished 7th in C major or minor can be transformed into a diminished 7th in E♭, F♯ or A (major or minor in each case) –

in C   in A   in F♯   in E♭

In this way, the chord offers considerable scope for modulation. Used as a pivot, it can be approached in one key and left in another. A passage from the first movement of Beethoven's 'Pathétique' Sonata provides a good illustration –

This extract starts in G minor, and the first three chords marked * are all diminished 7ths in that key (inversions of VII⁷). The fourth * chord sounds exactly the same as the second, but it is spelt differently: E♭ has become D♯.

Written in this way, it can be regarded as VII⁷d in E minor (D♯-F♯-A-C) or, more simply, as V⁷ – the C in the bass being an appoggiatura on to the root of the V⁷. It is worth noticing that although the diminished 7th chord here resolves into E minor it could also have resolved into E major. (In addition to the chords mentioned, there is also another diminished 7th chord: the one above the bass C♯ in the first bar. This is used as a chromatic chord resolving on to the dominant of G minor.)

Because it so easily suggests uncertainty of key, and because of the dissonances it contains, the diminished 7th chord can have a very restless quality. This effect is heightened when several diminished 7ths follow each other in descending semitones, e.g. –

Mozart used precisely these chords with brilliant effect in his Fantasia and Fugue in C (K.394) for piano. The passage (which is in free rhythm and without bar-lines) would take up too much space to quote in full, but the chords are laid out in wide arpeggios which all follow the pattern of the opening –

The last diminished 7th (on D♯) is followed by a ⁶₄ chord on E in A minor, so in spite of its many chromatic notes the passage ends where it began as regards key. (A similar succession of diminished 7th chords occurs in the closing bars of the Fantasia in Bach's Chromatic Fantasia and Fugue [BWV 903], although there it is used with quite different effect – supporting an elaborately expressive melody, and over a tonic pedal.)

The chord has often been used with great dramatic force in opera. Mozart again provides splendid examples – particularly towards the end of *Don Giovanni*. Two characters (first Donna Elvira and then Leporello) are both accompanied by diminished 7th chords as they cry out in horror when they catch sight of the statue of the murdered Commendatore approaching to summon Don Giovanni to hell. The actual entrance of the statue is marked by another diminished 7th chord (*ff*) –

This last diminished 7th, in fact, is not only important for its dramatic effect but also crucial for the musical structure of the entire opera, since it turns the music back to the tonic key of the entire work: D minor.

17/5 The augmented sixth

In the following pairs of examples, the chords marked * are identical –

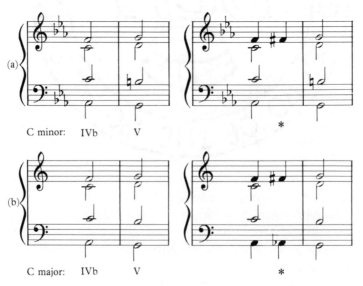

C minor: IVb   V

These chords have all arisen because accidentals have been introduced into a simple diatonic progression: IVb-V. In (a), F-G in the melody becomes F-F♯-G. The same thing happens in (b), but also the bass is changed: A-G becomes A-A♭-G. In (c), the normal resolution of the suspension (F) is changed to F♯.

A strongly dissonant harmonic interval is produced by the chromatic notes in these progressions: A♭-F♯. So striking is this interval that the chord itself is named after it – the **augmented sixth**. However, the augmented 6th chord occurs in three versions, and although all of these may be described as augmented 6th chords they also have individual names. All of them include the interval of a major 3rd as well as the augmented 6th above the bass note: e.g. . If only these three notes are used (as in the examples above), the chord is known as an **Italian sixth**. If an augmented 4th above the bass is added, e.g. , it becomes a **French sixth**; and if a perfect 5th above the bass is added, e.g. , it is a **German sixth**.

The augmented 6th chord originally arose as a result of chromatic notes moving by step, as illustrated by examples (a), (b) and (c). When, towards the end of the 18th century, it began to be treated as an independent chord (not merely as an elaboration of a diatonic progression), the chromatic notes were no longer always approached by step e.g. –

Being dissonant, the *interval* of the augmented 6th still expects a resolution. Normally the two notes open out to form an octave (or a compound octave) – , in which case the chord is commonly followed by V or by Ic-V, e.g. in C major or minor –

These quotations from Beethoven's piano music illustrate straightforward uses of augmented 6th chords –

Beethoven, Bagatelle, Op.119 No.1

G minor: It.6th

Beethoven, 'Pathétique' Sonata, (3rd mvt)

Eb major: Fr.6th

Beethoven, Piano Sonata, Op.109 (3rd mvt)

E major: Ger.6th

Augmented 6th chords are most frequently based on the minor 6th of the scale, as in all the illustrations given so far. But they are also sometimes used, both in major and in minor keys, on the minor 2nd (with corresponding resolutions on to I or IVc-I). This French 6th occurs in the orchestral introduction to Act I of Puccini's *La Bohème* –

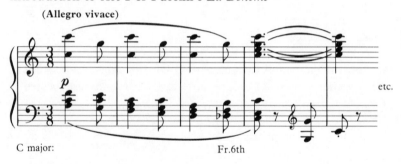

C major: Fr.6th

Occasionally augmented 6ths are based on other notes, for example the subdominant in major keys.

When the lower of the two notes forming the augmented 6th interval is in the bass, the chord is often described as being in 'root position'. This is certainly convenient, even though it is also somewhat illogical. (As the examples at the beginning of the section show, the bass note is not a root in the usual sense, i.e. it is not the foundation of a triad.) Similarly, and with similar reservations, the chord can be described as inverted when the lower note of the augmented 6th interval is not in the bass.

The following arrangements of three passages from the second movement of the Symphony No.1 by Brahms illustrate the use of 'inversions'. They are all in the tonic key of the movement: E major. (It is true that chromatic notes produce strong suggestions of E minor, but in context the impression is only temporary; moreover, the chords in question are the same in the minor as in the major.) All three passages include the German 6th on the minor 6th of the scale, but with different notes in the bass. At (a) the chord is in 'root position', at (b) in 'first inversion', and at (c) in 'second inversion' –

Like the diminished 7th, the augmented 6th chord has rich possibilities as a means of modulation. The most obvious example of this is the German 6th: spelt differently it becomes a V^7, e.g. –

German 6th
(e.g. on ♭VI in C) V^7 in D♭

Naturally, the Italian 6th – being identical with the German 6th but for the absence of one note – can function in the same way, e.g. –

Thus it is possible to modulate by means of a pivot chord which is a V^7 in one key but an augmented 6th in another. A very clear example occurs in the cadenza of the last movement of Mozart's C minor Piano Concerto –

The passage as quoted here starts in A♭ major. In the first bar there are two chords: Ic-V^7. The next bar sounds exactly the same, but the second chord is written differently. D♭ becomes C♯, and the chord thereby becomes an augmented (German) 6th chord. It is now treated as an augmented 6th on the minor 6th of the scale of G minor, and the passage continues in that key.

Another quotation from the opening chorus of *A German Requiem* by Brahms demonstrates a rather similar modulation. Before looking at the modulation itself it is worth noting what happens when the chorus enters at the beginning of the movement, which is in F major –

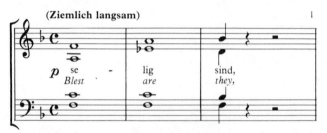

(Ziemlich langsam)   1

p   se   -   lig   sind,
Blest   *are*   *they,*

---

[1]In contexts such as this, it is not necessary to write four sets of rests – one for each voice (SATB). One set per stave is sufficient to make clear what is intended.

The first bar here consists of a tonic chord. The second bar adds a minor 7th to the tonic chord, so that it can act as a secondary dominant to the next chord (bar 3), which is IVc in F. This is all relevant to the modulation in question, which occurs a few pages further on. Here the music is in Db major (see p.148), and the chorus re-enters with its opening theme, but now in Db. One expects it to continue in the same way, i.e.

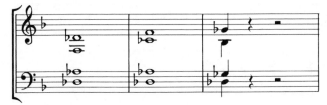

But what actually happens is this –

The fact that the inner parts have been interchanged in bar 1 is of no consequence – the chord is still I (in Db). However, the re-writing of Cb as B♮ is of great significance: the chord is transformed into a German 6th. In this form it can now lead the music back to its home key, F major. It is treated as an augmented 6th on the bVI in F, followed by Ic. (The orchestra then takes over this Ic chord and continues in F major.)

The scope for modulation is widened much further when one takes account of the fact that the augmented 6th can be based not only on bVI but on other notes of the scale as well – e.g. on bII and on IV. It could be approached as an augmented 6th on bVI in C, for example, and left as an augmented 6th on bII in G, or on IV in Eb (or, of course, vice versa in each case).

17/6 Harmonic sequences

A **sequence** is a pattern of notes which is immediately repeated at a higher or lower pitch. There may be only one repetition, or several. Sequences may occur in a melodic line ('melodic' sequences) or in the chords used ('harmonic' sequences): the two can be used independently, although usually they are combined. This section deals with harmonic sequences.[1]

[1]See 18/3 concerning melodic sequences.

By far the most common kind of harmonic sequence is one in which each chord is followed by one whose root is a 4th higher or (which comes to the same thing) a 5th lower. The following example represents the basic pattern. (For ease of reference and comparison, this outline and the variations of it which occur later will be given in C major and lettered (a), (b), etc. No special significance need be attached to the time signature or its strong–weak implications: the progressions can be differently accented and, of course, used with different rhythms.)

A 7th may be added to alternate chords, or to every chord, without the basic progression being affected, e.g. –

There is an example of the use of pattern (c) in the third movement of Mozart's Piano Sonata, K.533, (although, because of the three-part texture, the 5th from the root is absent from each chord) –

This passage is simply an elaboration of –

F minor: I   IV⁷   ♭VII⁷   III⁷   VI⁷   II⁷   V⁷

(Note the 7ths and their resolutions, indicated by arrows.)

The pattern outlined at (a) may be modified by the use of inversions, with or without 7ths, e.g. –

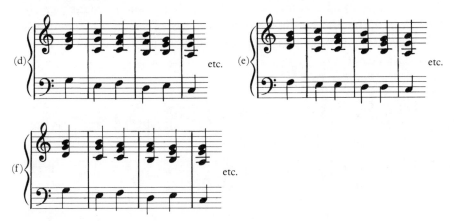

All the above sequences are entirely diatonic. As a direct consequence, the opening chord progression in each case is not always followed absolutely exactly. In (a), for instance, the first three chords are all major, but the fourth chord is diminished, while the next three are all minor. Notice, too, that one interval in the bass line is not perfect: F-B is a diminished 5th.

When the repetitions of the opening pattern are transposed *exactly*, a sequence is said to be 'real'. Here, for example, are the first three chords at (a) continued as a real sequence –

The other sequences can similarly be turned into real sequences: e.g. (b) becomes –

Sequences such as (g) and (h) above, it will be noticed, are simply successions of V-I progressions in keys descending in whole tones: C major, B♭ major, A♭ major, and so on. Real sequences, therefore, are a means of modulation. They can be kept going just long enough to get from one key to the next (e.g. from C to B♭ in the last two examples – the first four chords of each), or they can be continued further to reach more distant keys. An example of the latter occurs in the first movement of Schubert's Piano Sonata in E, where the composer uses the pattern outlined in (h) to modulate from B major to F major –

There is no necessity, however, for sequences to be either diatonic or real. This can be illustrated by comparing a different sequence with two variations of it –

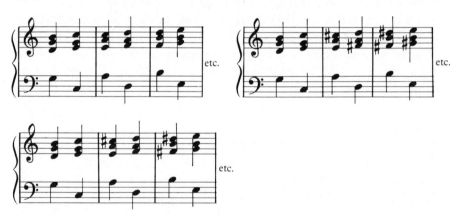

The first of these patterns is diatonic; the second real – a succession of V-I progressions in C major, D major, E major. The third, however, is neither diatonic nor real: it is a succession of V-I progressions in C major, D *minor* and E *minor*.[1] A passage employing this last pattern (but with the addition of a 7th to each of the V chords) is to be found in the second movement of Beethoven's Piano Sonata, Op.14 No.2 –

[1]This type of sequence is perhaps best called a 'tonal' sequence, although purely diatonic sequences are also said to be 'tonal'. Another term, 'modulating sequence', is usually reserved for a sequence which leads to a change of key (as in the Schubert example above), and hence can exclude sequences of the present type – as will be seen in the Beethoven example which follows.

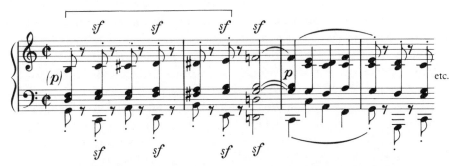

A striking feature of this passage is the way in which the melody moves up in semitones. The chromatic ascent can be moved to the bass part by varying the same sequence with alternate chords in first inversion –

If the bracketed accidentals are included, the sequence becomes real. We have already seen an example of this progression in the extract from Handel's *Messiah* on p.152.

In the Beethoven quotation above, it is important to notice that the passage ends where it began: in C major. Indeed, it can accurately be said to be in C throughout. The 7th chords on the bass notes A and B (bars 1–2) are simply chromatic chords in C major – secondary dominants leading respectively to the diatonic chords of II and III.

Even real sequences do not always modulate *into* the keys which they touch – not even temporarily. Here, for example, is a further variation of (a) above: it should be compared with (h) –

In this progression, the first chord is the dominant 7th of C major. The listener expects it to be followed by a tonic chord in C major, but a 7th (B♭) has been added to the C major chord so that it becomes instead the dominant 7th of F major. This chord is in turn followed by the dominant 7th of B♭ major . . . and so on. No chord, in fact, can be taken as a tonic: the whole progression is

simply a sequence of dominant 7ths. One can say that it modulates from
C major 'through' F major, Bb major, Eb major, Ab major etc., but not that it
modulates *into* any of them. However long it is continued, it will not arrive *in* a
key until the sequence itself is brought to an end and emerges on what can be
taken as a tonic chord.

All the sequences discussed so far have been sequences derived from two
chords. The two quotations which follow are examples of more extended
sequences. The first is derived from three chords; the second from four (as
shown by the given chord indications). Both are tonal sequences –

Weber, *Der Freischütz* (Overture)

C minor: I
Eb major: VI   V   I
G minor: VI   V   I
Bb major: VI   V^(7)   I

Beethoven, Piano Sonata, Op.10 No.1 (1st mvt)

Ab major: V⁷d   Ib   V⁷c   I   F minor: V⁷d

Ib   V⁷c   I Db major: V⁷d   Ib   V⁷c   I

CHAPTER 18

Aspects of melody

18/1 Some definitions

At its simplest, **melody** can be defined as a pattern of different notes performed one after another, i.e. one at a time. The pattern is formed by the pitches of the notes and by their rhythms. In most of the music which is familiar to us, melody is designed to go with harmony, and is closely related to it. But it has to be remembered that melody can perfectly well exist by itself – without harmony or, indeed, any kind of accompaniment.[1] Most folksongs were conceived without harmony, and so, of course, was all music composed before harmony had been invented. After the invention of harmony, professional composers very rarely wrote unaccompanied melody – not, at least, until around the end of the 19th century, since when some outstanding examples have been written (e.g. Debussy's *Syrinx*, for solo flute).

When we talk about 'a melody', or about 'melodies', we mean rather more than when we talk about 'melody' alone. A melody is melody shaped in a particular way: shaped so that it seems musically complete, and with a clear sense of inner design. (There is no real difference between a melody and a 'tune', although the latter word is often used to describe a melody which is especially clear-cut and memorable.) The design of a melody or tune is provided by the ways in which the phrases relate to each other. For example, they may all be the same length; or a rising or falling pattern of notes in one phrase may be imitated in another, either exactly or approximately. Later in this chapter we shall explore these issues in some detail, but first we must consider a more general aspect of melody: the pitches of the notes, and the ways in which one note moves to another.

[1] Melody by itself – i.e without harmony, and not combined with other melodies to make counterpoint – is known technically as 'monophony' (from the Greek for 'single sound'). Compare 'homophony' and 'polyphony' (see footnote on p.126). The word 'monody' (from the Greek for 'single song') refers to *sung* melody: modern composers sometimes use it to describe an unaccompanied melody for solo voice, but the word is more commonly applied to certain types of accompanied song, particularly in Italian music of the early 17th century.

18/2 Note relationships

The earliest melodies were sung, and our notions of melody – of what is 'melodic' or 'melodious' – have continued to be greatly influenced by what is easily singable. This, at its most basic, is a purely practical matter. For example, the voice has only a limited range, and so we very soon run up against the problem of notes that are too high or too low. Similarly, the voice does not easily adjust between two notes which are far apart in pitch, which makes it difficult for us to manage leaps of very wide intervals. But there is a deeper issue: to be able to sing a note one has first to 'hear' it. This means in effect that one has to be able to relate it mentally to the previous note. If there is no clear relationship, we have considerable difficulty. The usual way in which notes of a melody are related is that they all belong to a particular scale. Even then, however, we tend to find some intervals awkward, especially augmented and diminished intervals.

As harmony became established, people grew accustomed to the sound of chords. Consequently, melodic patterns made from the notes of chords became easy to 'take in' and therefore to sing – even if they included several leaps in succession. There is no great difficulty in singing this, for example, because all the notes belong to a major chord –

Similarly, these notes all belong to a dominant 7th chord –

and so can quite easily be 'placed' in the mind – even the diminished 5th between the E and the B♭. But augmented and diminished intervals which are *not* related as notes of a chord are still likely to seem difficult. Just one accidental added to the last example would be sufficient to destroy its chord pattern, thereby making it far more hazardous to sing –

Not only is there a problem in 'finding' the augmented 5th (C-G♯), but the diminished 5th (E-B♭) also becomes troublesome because the sense of a familiar chord has been lost.

Of course, passages which would be difficult – or even impossible – to sing may not be at all difficult to *play*. Most instruments have a much wider range than the voice, and some (e.g. the clarinet and the violin) are particularly well adapted to patterns such as wide leaps. And on many instruments (notably keyboard instruments) one does not have to be able to 'hear' a note before one can play it. Nevertheless, even melodic passages written for instruments regularly display many features which are also found in those written for the voice. Sometimes this is simply because we find anything which we can associate with singing particularly expressive and eloquent (hence the frequency of the direction *cantabile*). But there is another reason. As listeners, we can very well grasp patterns in instrumental music which are similar to common patterns in vocal music, even if they could not literally be sung. This passage, for example, is too high to sing, yet we feel entirely at home with it since it would be easily singable if it were one or two octaves lower.

In much the same way, when we hear this extract from the first movement of the Clarinet Sonata in F minor by Brahms (played by a B♭ clarinet and quoted as written – i.e. at the transposed pitch[1]) –

we have no difficulty in understanding the pattern in the notes marked ⌐ *x* ¬ , even though they could scarcely be sung. We instinctively recognise that they all belong to a straightforward chord, one which frequently gives rise to equivalent patterns in vocal melody.

Both vocal and instrumental melody, indeed, can be largely built out of chord patterns. A very clear example occurs in a passage at the beginning of Schubert's Symphony No.5, in B♭, starting at bar 5 –

[1]See p.211.

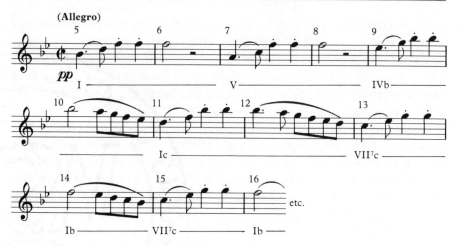

Bars 5, 7, 9, 11, 13 and 15 are made exclusively from the notes of ordinary diatonic triads in Bb. In fact, the entire harmony of this particular extract can be said to be outlined in the melody, as can be seen by comparing the chords actually used by the composer (indicated below the staves).

18/3 Melodic sequences

It was pointed out earlier (at the beginning of 17/6) that melodic and harmonic sequences are very frequently combined. Thus, some of the quotations which were given as examples of harmonic sequences also provide examples of melodic sequences: notice particularly the extracts from Mozart (on p.166), Weber and Beethoven (p.170).

It was also noted that melodic and harmonic sequences can be used independently. In this passage, for instance, there is a melodic sequence, but no harmonic sequence –

Bach, French Suite No.2 (Minuet)

Here the sequence is diatonic: it does not modulate, but neither is the transposition exact. (An exact transposition – i.e. a real sequence – would have required Bbs in the second bar of the melody.) Further melodic sequences, again diatonic, are to be found in bars 7–9 of the Wagner quotation on p.187.

18/4 Regular phrases

The most common type of phrase is four bars long. A typical phrase in $\frac{4}{4}$, therefore, would contain 16 beats; one in $\frac{3}{4}$ would contain 12 beats, and so on. Often such phrases start at the beginning of bar 1 and finish at the end of bar 4, for example –

However, the 16 beats could be grouped differently: they do not always start at the beginning of a bar e.g. –

We have seen in Part I (p.68) how a phrase of this kind may be set to a line of poetry. And just as a line of verse creates an expectation of another line to follow it, so a musical phrase seems to demand another, matching phrase. Two phrases working together like this may be compared to a question and an answer. Technically they are called an **antecedent** and a **consequent**, the two together forming a **sentence**.[1]

Even the shortest melody must have at least two phrases: an antecedent and a consequent. Below is an example (again from the first movement of Schubert's 5th Symphony). Although it occurs during the course of a long movement, it is nevertheless a true melody, complete in itself.

[1] In a song, a musical sentence does not necessarily correspond with a sentence in the words, so the full stops in the words cannot be taken as a guide to the phrase structure! (Some writers use the word 'period' to describe a musical sentence, but that word is also used in more general senses.)

It is not just that these phrases are the same length which makes them seem to
belong to each other: their rhythms are almost identical. Moreover, there are
two other features which contribute to the question-and-answer effect. The
first is provided by the pitch-patterns in the melody: the opening six notes are
repeated almost exactly at the beginning of the second phrase, although
transposed one note higher. The second feature is to be found in the
accompanying harmony. As quoted above, the melody is in Bb major,[1] ending
on the tonic, and harmonised by a perfect cadence in that key. In the middle,
however, it modulates briefly into C minor; and the first phrase ends with a C
minor chord (II in Bb). Clearly the music could not finish at this point. The
harmony too demands an answering phrase, one which will bring it back to the
tonic of the home key: Bb. Other features (such as dynamics) can also
contribute to the feeling of phrase structure in music, but the above example
illustrates the three which are most crucial: rhythm, pitch-patterns in the
melody, and (in harmonised music) the accompanying harmonies.

An antecedent may be followed by more than one consequent. At the
beginning of Beethoven's Piano Sonata in F, Op.10 No.2, for instance, there
are three phrases: an antecedent plus two consequents –

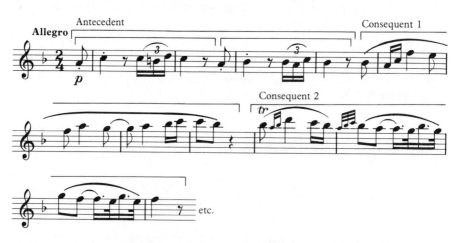

Phrases sometimes (though not always) divide into smaller passages called
sections. The first phrase of the last quotation is an example, made clear by
the rhythmic repetition (shown by brackets enclosed within the phrase
brackets). In the next quotation below, both phrases divide into sections –

---

[1] At its first appearance in the movement, it was in the dominant key (F). It is quoted here as it
occurs later, in the tonic key. In the score, the melody is doubled an octave lower by the 2nd
violins, and the bass line is doubled an octave lower by the double basses.

Allegro   Mozart, Piano Sonata, K.576 (1st mvt)

Here the antecedent and the consequent are almost identical in their first sections: their rhythms are exactly the same, and both are formed from the notes of chords (I in the first section of the first phrase, and II in the first section of the second phrase). Notice the importance of the two cadences (imperfect at the end of the first phrase, perfect at the end of the second) in producing the question-and-answer effect.

There are two other basic points to note concerning phrases. The first is that two phrases may be linked by decorative notes following the cadence at the end of the first phrase. Two 2-bar phrases are linked in the next example –

Adagio   Mozart, Piano Sonata, K.570 (2nd mvt)
(link)

If the linking notes are omitted, the balance of the music is not affected, but the basic structure is easier to see –

The other point is this: the length of a phrase cannot always be assessed simply by the total number of beats its melody may happen to contain. A 4-bar phrase in a $\frac{4}{4}$ melody, for example, does not necessarily contain exactly 16 beats. This can be illustrated by the following quotation: the opening of a song (from *Frauenliebe und -leben*) by Schumann. Although it is a sentence consisting of two 4-bar phrases (after a 1-bar introduction), the second phrase in the voice part appears to start early, taking a beat from the end of the phrase before it –

Au – ge,   hel–ler Sinn und fe – ster Muth.
spark –ling,   brave in heart and strong_ in   mind.

etc.

The harmonic rhythm, however, is crucial in this passage: the change of harmony occurs punctually on the first beat of bar 6. (Bar 5 is I throughout, with the F's in the treble clef as non-harmony notes suspended from the previous chord; and the first two beats of bar 6 are V, the E♭ in the bass being a suspension.) What actually determines the length of a phrase is the number of 'strong' beats it includes – meaning, in this connection, the number of beats which occur as the first beat of a bar.

18/5 Design in melodies

The last section has already broached the subject of melodic design by considering the simplest patterns: melodies consisting of two 4-bar phrases. What follows now is an introduction to more extended and elaborate designs. Melodies of more than two phrases tend to divide into multiples of two, e.g. –

    16-bar melodies consisting of four 4-bar phrases
    24-bar melodies consisting of six 4-bar phrases
    32-bar melodies consisting of four 8-bar phrases

A vocal example of a 16-bar melody, 'Sweet Polly Oliver', was quoted in Part I (p.68). Here is an instrumental example: the waltz in the second movement ('A Ball') of the *Fantastic Symphony* by Berlioz –

The melody begins on the third quaver of bar 1 and consists of two phrases, the break between them occurring in the middle of bar 9. (As in the Schumann song discussed earlier, bar 1 is really an introduction: the two semiquavers form an anacrusis to bar 2, which is where the phrase begins as regards its harmonic rhythm.) The two phrases in the second sentence are slightly varied versions of those in the first: a plan which can be represented by the formula ABAB. Both sentences end with a perfect cadence. Note, however, that the effect of the first is slightly less final because the melody comes to rest (bar 9) on the third of the tonic chord, not on its root (as in bar 17).

A well-known March by Sousa, *The Stars and Stripes Forever*, provides a very straightforward example of a 32-bar melody (in A♭ major) consisting of four 8-bar phrases –

To save space, only the melody has been quoted; but an important feature of its accompanying harmony is that phrases 1 and 2 end with dominant chords, and phrase 3 (which includes a passing modulation to F minor) with VI[1]. Each of the phrases falls into two equal sections (particularly noticeable because of the long note in the middle of each phrase).

Melodies of 8, 16 or 32 bars are the most common. Those of other lengths are slightly more complicated in their organisation, even when made out of regular 4-bar phrases. The *Ode to Joy* melody, from the last movement of Beethoven's 9th Symphony, for example, has a total of 24 bars, divided into six 4-bar phrases (three antecedent + consequent groups). At its first appearance the melody is unaccompanied, played by cellos and double basses –

[1]The B♭ is an appoggiatura to the 3rd of the F minor chord.

Phrases 1, 2, 4 and 6 are virtually the same; phrases 3 and 5 provide a contrast, but are identical with each other. Thus the overall plan could be represented as AABABA. Although Beethoven chose to write the melody out in full, it could have been written with repeat marks – AA ‖:BA:‖ .

The next example *does* use repeat marks. It could be represented thus – AB :‖: A¹AA² :‖ . The third and fifth phrases have been denoted as A¹ and A² because, although their rhythms are almost the same as that of the first phrase, their notes are strikingly different.

Presto ma non troppo   Haydn, Piano Sonata, Hob.XVI/37 (Finale)

Some points in the harmony reinforce the overall plan:

Phrase 1 (A) ends on the tonic chord (I in D)
Phrase 2 (B) ends on V (a temporary modulation to the dominant key)
Phrase 3 (A¹) ends on V
Phrase 4 (A) ends on I
Phrase 5 (A²) ends on I

The varied A phrases contain hints of other modulations: A¹ to E minor, and A² to G major (though the latter is only apparent in the left-hand part, not included here).

18/6 Irregular phrases

Phrase patterns of the kind discussed earlier in this chapter have always been common – and still are – in dances, marches, simple songs etc. They were even more widely used by classical composers and by the many later composers who continued classical traditions. Nevertheless, even in the works of classical composers there were exceptions. These, for instance, are two musical sentences by Mozart which do *not* divide into 4- or 8-bar phrases –

5-bar phrases:

6-bar phrases:

In each of these, the consequent is the same length as the antecedent (5 + 5 and 6 + 6 bars). To this extent, there is a feeling of balance in both of them.

But in other types of music, and in music of other periods, more flexible phrase patterns are common: not only more varied phrase lengths but also phrases which do not combine to form antecedent + consequent pairs. In these circumstances there may be little purpose in describing a phrase as 'irregular'. A phrase can only be felt to be irregular if it occurs where a regular phrase might have been expected – for example, where a 4-bar antecedent is followed by a consequent which does *not* match it in length. This happens at the opening of a violin piece, 'Tempo di Minuetto', by the great violinist Kreisler[1]: a 4-bar antecedent is followed by a 9-bar consequent –

[1]He originally published it under the pseudonym 'Pugnani'.

An irregular consequent can be the result of expanding what is basically a regular phrase. One way of achieving this expansion is by 'interpolation', i.e. the addition of extra music in the middle of the phrase. There is a clear example in the second movement of Mozart's Piano Sonata, K.330. Only the melody can be quoted here, but the sonata itself should be consulted if possible.[1]

The interpolated section (in bars 14–18) has been enclosed in square brackets. A lesser composer might simply have left this out, producing thereby the expected 4-bar phrase. This would have 'worked' perfectly well (as can be seen by playing the passage without including the bracketed section) – but at what a loss!

As this last example shows, a phrase lengthened by interpolation can give a feeling of great breadth. The effect is achieved precisely because a regular

[1]Readers who have the Mozart Piano Sonatas should notice that, apart from the phrase in question and its repetition later, this entire movement consists of regular 4-bar phrases. Similar, though rather more complex, examples of interpolation occur in the Sonata K.533: the first 22 bars of the second movement.

phrase – or a succession of regular phrases – has led the listener to expect another regular phrase to complete the pattern; yet when the consequent phrase is reached, it does not finish as expected. The listener is made to wait for its completion.

There are other ways of extending what would otherwise be a regular phrase. For example, instead of a perfect cadence at the expected time there may be an interrupted cadence, the perfect cadence being delayed until later. Or the time values of the closing notes may be doubled – making, in effect, a written-out *ritenuto*. Examples of these two devices can be found respectively in bars 1–10 of Schumann's 'Erinnerung' (No.28 in *Album for the Young*), and at the end of the solo part in 'O rest in the Lord' from Mendelssohn's *Elijah*.

It is rather rare for a 4-bar phrase to be answered by a phrase of *less* than four bars. But something of the same effect is produced when two phrases overlap – i.e the end of one becomes the beginning of another. Again a slow movement in Mozart's Piano Sonatas offers a memorable example: the opening of the second movement of K.311.

This consists of three phrases: an antecedent followed by two consequents. All are 4-bar phrases, and everything is quite regular until the end of the second phrase (the G in bar 8); but then one becomes aware that another phrase has already started. As well as being the last note of the second phrase, the G is also the first note of the third phrase. This last phrase finishes with the first note of bar 12 (or, when the repeat is made, with the first note of bar 1 – producing another overlap).

18/7 Motifs

A musical **figure** is a very short musical idea. It could even be as short as two notes. A figure which becomes a distinctive and important feature of the music is a **motif**[1]. When it recurs, a motif is generally modified – especially in the pitch-pattern of its notes, which may be quite substantially varied. Its rhythm (which in most cases is its most striking characteristic) is less frequently changed, and usually less radically. The ⌐‾‾‾¬ marks in these quotations indicate examples –

(In bars 11–12, the basic motif – shown by asterisks – has been elaborated.)

As these extracts show, motifs can be important constituents of melody. But they also have a much wider use, particularly in music with a more complicated texture than a single melodic line supported by accompanying

---

[1] 'Motif' is a more precise word than 'motive', though the latter is often used in this context with the same meaning.

harmonies. What must surely be the most celebrated example of the development of a motif is to be found in the subsequent adventures of the motif which opens Beethoven's 5th Symphony. This is only the beginning –

The next quotation, the opening of the first of J. S. Bach's Inventions for keyboard, illustrates the use of a motif in a piece which is exclusively contrapuntal –

The complete piece is almost entirely built out of the motif provided by its first eight notes. Sometimes (e.g. the right-hand notes in bar 3) its 'inversion' is used – meaning that ascending intervals become descending intervals and vice versa.[1] Sometimes only its first four notes are used, but in doubled time values,[2] e.g. the left-hand notes in bars 3–6 marked [⌐⎯⎯⎯⎯⎯¬]. The same device is also used in a decorated form in bar 6 (the notes marked *).

Bach is particularly associated with the best-known and largest category of contrapuntal compositions based on a short melodic idea: the fugue. In a fugue, this idea is called the **subject**[3]. Usually there is at least one other, contrasted idea, the **counter-subject**, with which it can be combined. But even this can be dispensed with if the subject itself contains sufficient material. This happens, for example, in the D major fugue in Book II of Bach's '48', where the subject, although brief, contains two distinct motifs, which between them provide the essential material for the entire piece –

[1] This type of inversion – 'melodic' inversion – is not to be confused with 'harmonic' inversion: the inversion of intervals, triads and chords (see Part I, pp.54–5, 58 & 60).

[2] Lengthening the time values of notes in a melodic passage is called 'augmentation' (again not to be confused with the augmentation of intervals, triads and chords – see Part I, pp.48, 57 & 60). Usually the time values are doubled, as here. The Wagner quotation on p.187 contains further examples. Similarly, shortening the time values of notes is called 'diminution'.

[3] In other musical contexts (notably in sonata-form movements by classical and later composers), the word 'subject' has a somewhat different meaning – still implying a principal musical idea, but one which is much more extensive and which normally includes harmony as well as melody.

18/8 The bass line

When a melody or a melodic passage is the main point of interest in a musical passage, it is usually at the top of the music (as, for instance, in the example by Berlioz on p.180); although it can sometimes be found in the middle of the texture (see the Schubert quotation on p.131), or in the bass –

The bass still has a special significance, however, even when it does not carry the main melodic interest. This is just as important when it is settled on one note as when it is moving. A tonic pedal, for example, is a common way of firmly establishing the sense of the tonic as 'home' at the beginning of a long movement. (One by Beethoven is quoted on p.125.) Most of the time, of course, the bass does move, though often changing its notes less frequently than the melody does. Since it has a special importance in the harmony, the bass has a tendency to move in particular ways. Its most characteristic move from one note to another is a leap of a perfect 4th or a perfect 5th, either up or down. This is because the commonest type of strong harmonic progression is produced by two chords whose roots are a 4th or a 5th apart (as, for example, in perfect and plagal cadences). The progression is at its strongest when both chords are in root position. Two quotations will illustrate the point. The first is the opening of the slow movement of Beethoven's 'Emperor' Concerto, played by muted strings with the bass line *pizzicato* –

(In the last bar, the intervening Ib chord does not remove the strength of the move from I to V.) The second quotation is from Chopin's C minor Prelude for piano, Op.28 No.20 –

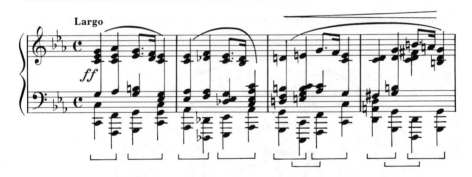

Leaps of a 4th or a 5th (or, indeed, of wider intervals) in a bass part can have a strong effect even when the notes are not the bass of $\frac{5}{3}$ chords. The two chords marked * in this harmonisation by Bach (the opening of the so-called 'Passion Chorale') are examples –

Naturally, a bass part which consisted of nothing but leaps would quickly become monotonous and angular, e.g. –

This bass merely moves up and down mechanically (a type of movement sometimes compared to that of a bicycle pump!). The difference between it and Bach's bass is that his has a real sense of shaping and melodic purpose. Yet Bach's bass is nevertheless a characteristically 'bass' phrase: its purely harmonic function is not compromised, and it would sound improbable as a soprano melody.

Bach made many harmonisations of the same chorale melody[1], but in all of them the bass has the same qualities. Here are the openings of two more –

In his C minor Prelude, Chopin also provided a contrast to leaps in the bass. After the passage quoted on p.191 (bars 1–4), the bass continues by gradually easing itself down, step by step, in bars 5–6:

A bass part slowly moving up or down a scale, either diatonic or chromatic, is a powerful means of holding the music together. But it can contribute more than that: it can be a powerful means of expression. The C minor Prelude has an air of solemnity from the beginning, but the chromatic passage in bars 5–6 tempers it with a more melancholy, wistful feeling. It is no coincidence that this particular bass – a chromatic descent from the tonic to the dominant below – has often been associated with grief. Two of the most celebrated

---

[1] – five of them in the *St Matthew Passion*. It is not, however, always sung to the same words; nor is it always in the same key. The last version quoted here has been transposed up a tone for ease of comparison.

examples come from the baroque period: 'Dido's Lament' from Purcell's *Dido and Aeneas*, and the 'Crucifixus' from Bach's B Minor Mass. In both cases, a bass pattern is repeated over and over again – a device called a **ground bass** or '*basso ostinato*'. The Purcell example begins as follows (only the solo voice part and the bass are given) –

Contrariwise, a bass which moves *up* a scale can produce an effect of mounting excitement. Mozart used this device with immense dramatic effect in Act II of *Don Giovanni*, shortly after the passage quoted on p.160. The Commendatore's exhortation to Don Giovanni (beginning with the words 'Tu m'invitasti a ceno') becomes increasingly tense and urgent through being set to a slowly rising chromatic scale in the bass. Quite different in style, but no less powerful, is a passage in Bach's Fantasia in G for organ, BWV 572: in this case it is a diatonic scale which contributes to the building-up of tension as it slowly climbs up two whole octaves –

18/9 Outlined melody

In music written for instruments – particularly keyboard instruments, and
most of all the piano – melodic passages are often decorated in ways which
make them not immediately obvious when written down. A passage from
Handel's keyboard Fantasia in C, HWV 490, provides a simple illustration –

The semiquavers conceal what are essentially melodic phrases moving in quavers and by step: they are a variation of this –

With the passing of time, decorations which were similar in principle became more elaborate, as in the following extract from the Intermezzo in A minor for piano by Brahms (Op.116 No.2) –

Here, the right hand is tracing out a melody at two different levels, an octave apart: the melody is in effect being played in octaves, although the notes of the octaves are sounded alternately, not simultaneously. Brahms himself left a simplified version, in which the basic melody (the beamed quavers) is easier to see –

Another look at the Handel example quoted earlier will confirm that a bass line can be similarly fragmented. In this connection, it is important to stress that in music of the tonal period there virtually *always* is a bass line, since there is always harmony. This is no less true in music which at first glance is not even chordal. The next quotation illustrates the point. It is the opening of the

Courante from Bach's Partita No.1, in B minor, for unaccompanied solo violin –

Although the bass line is merely outlined by the lowest note of each bar, it is nevertheless the foundation of a full harmonic progression. Moreover, it has a feeling of melodic continuity and shape. This is easier to see in the following rearrangement of the passage, where the bass is given in full-size notes, with small-size notes above to show the essentials of the harmonies –

The outlining of a bass part is very common in romantic piano music. An example by Brahms was quoted on p.131 in connection with part-writing. Here is a more elaborate example, from the first movement of Rachmaninov's Piano Concerto No.2 (notice the stepwise movement in both passages) –

Despite the fact that it is accompanied, this passage could equally well have occurred in a piece written for piano alone. The orchestral instruments add nothing essential: all they do is to sustain the basic chords in long-held notes. Especially interesting in the present context, however, is the music played by the second bassoon and the double basses together; for what this shows clearly is the full implications of the lowest notes played by the piano, i.e. the true bass line of the music –

CHAPTER 19

String instruments

19/1 Orchestral strings

The so-called 'strings' of string instruments are in fact made of gut, wire or nylon. Any such string will produce a musical note when it is made to vibrate. What determines the pitch of the note is (a) the tension and (b) the length of the string: tightening a string and shortening it will both make it produce a higher note. (The thickness of a string also affects its pitch, but that is a matter which concerns manufacturers rather than players.) When the player of an instrument such as a violin 'tunes' the instrument before playing, it is the *tension* which is being adjusted. Each string has a peg by means of which it can be tightened or slackened until exactly the required note is produced. When the instrument is actually played, however, the player is in effect constantly varying the *length* of the strings. The string is pressed against the body of the instrument (the part called the 'finger board') so that it cannot vibrate along its full length: the section which is left free to vibrate is shorter and the sound therefore higher. Naturally the player has to judge precisely where to press or 'stop' the string according to which note is required.

A string which is not stopped in this way is said to be 'open'. The open note is therefore the lowest note it can produce. All the string instruments in the orchestra have four strings, and their open strings are tuned thus –

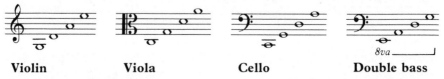

| Violin | Viola | Cello | Double bass |

Cello is an abbreviation for violoncello (N.B. not 'violincello'). Some double basses have a fifth string tuned to the B or C below the bottom E, or – increasingly common – a mechanism attached to the E string which enables the semitones down to C to be produced. It is impossible to fix an upper limit for the violin or any of the other instruments, since everything depends upon the skill of the player. But given good players, one can expect a range of about 3½ octaves from all of them except the double bass, where a little under three is more probable.

Normally the four instruments use the clefs shown above, but for its highest notes the viola may use the treble clef instead. Similarly, the cello may use the tenor clef, and even the treble clef. (Classical composers such as Haydn, Mozart and Beethoven used to write cello passages in the treble clef an octave higher than they actually sound, but this pointless custom no longer prevails.) The double bass may also use the tenor clef and, very rarely, the treble clef. But whatever clef it uses, the double bass always sounds an octave lower than written: the *8va* sign used in the above table is taken for granted in practice and is never actually shown.

It frequently happens that a particular note can be produced by more than one string. The colour of the note's sound varies slightly when it is produced by different strings. Consequently, if a composer wishes to specify that a particular string be used, this is indicated by 'sul A', 'sul E' etc. (*sul* is Italian for 'on the'). Strings can also be designated by Roman numerals, the highest being the first (I): for example, the French direction 'IIe corde' (= *deuxième corde*, i.e. second string) has the same meaning as 'sul A' when applied to the violin.

When two notes in succession are played on the same string, the player usually stops them with two different fingers. But the same finger may be used for both – by simply sliding it along the string from one position to the other. Although this can be done very quickly, the two notes are perceptibly linked by a gliding effect in the sound. The sound is 'carried' from one note to the other – which is the meaning of the Italian term for this technique: *portamento*. The technique is often used without any explicit direction in the music, but it can be ensured by a line drawn between the two notes, e.g.

19/2 Bowing

To make a string vibrate it can either be played with a 'bow' (a stick with horsehair tightly stretched along it) or plucked with the fingers. Violins and the other instruments mentioned normally use bows (though not the double bass when it is used in jazz). If, however, they are to be plucked, the music is marked **pizzicato** or, more commonly, just *pizz*. The word **arco** means that the bow is to be used again.

Bow strokes may be 'down' or 'up', i.e. moving from the 'heel' of the bow (the end which is held) to the 'point' (the far end), or in the opposite direction. Down and up bows are indicated by the signs ⊓ and ∨ respectively, placed above the notes. Two or more notes within a slur are played 'in one bow', i.e. in a single bow stroke, either up or down. This may be illustrated by further reference to the *Gavotta* in Prokofiev's *Classical Symphony*. When quoted on p.69 in Part I, square brackets were used to indicate the phrase structure.

What Prokofiev actually showed, however, was the bowing and articulation required, as in this phrase –

Here the first note is to be played with a down bow; the C♯ and B quavers are played in one bow – an up bow; the A and G quavers are played in one down bow; the F♯ is an up bow, and the following crotchets are played with alternate down and up bows.

Single bow strokes can be played in many different ways, with varying degrees of legato, staccato and pressure. String players know these bowing techniques by an assortment of French and Italian words, e.g. *détaché*, *louré*, *martelé*, *spiccato* and *saltando*. These terms, however, need not detain a non-player since they are rarely used as directions in the music itself: the appropriate style of bowing is deduced (as in the above example) from ⊓ and V directions, slurs and conventional articulation signs.

Alternating bow strokes played as quickly as possible on single notes are called a 'bowed *tremolo*'. They are shown by three strokes through the stems of the notes if they are minims or crotchets, two if they are quavers, and one if they are semiquavers. Semibreves have three strokes drawn above or below them –

An extra stroke and/or the word *tremolo* (or *trem.*) may be added if there is any danger of this notation being misunderstood as reiterated, measured notes (see p.99 in Part I), as might happen at very slow speeds.

The Italian direction *sul ponticello* means that the bow is to be played as close as possible to the bridge (the wooden support for the strings) in order to produce a rather thin, wiry sound. *Naturale* then indicates that the ordinary position is to be resumed, i.e. with the bow a little further down the strings. *Col legno* is the Italian instruction to turn the bow over and play the string (usually by tapping it) with the wood instead of with the hair, thus producing a dry, spooky effect. The return to normal bowing is marked *arco*. More common is the use of a mute, a device placed on the bridge to dampen the sound. This too is shown by an Italian direction in the music: *con sordino* or *con sordini* (both usually abbreviated as *con sord.*), meaning 'with mute(s)'. Similarly, *senza sord.* means 'without mute(s)'.

19/3 Multiple stops

It is possible for the bow to engage two adjacent strings simultaneously. Notes produced in this way are called **double stops**. The effect of three- or four-part chords can also be produced: the bow is drawn very rapidly across the strings from the lowest upwards. When this happens, however, only the top one or two notes can be sustained, since the bow cannot *remain* in contact with

more than two strings. Consequently, although might be written,

it would be played or .

19/4 Harmonics

It was explained at the beginning of this chapter that the length of a string is one of the factors which determine the pitch of the note produced. A string vibrates in a complicated way, not merely throughout its entire length but in smaller segments: halves, thirds, quarters etc. The places on the string where these subdivisions occur are called **nodes**. The subsidiary vibrations produce faint, independent notes called **overtones** or **harmonics**, at fixed intervals (an octave, 12th etc.) above the main (**fundamental**) note. Normally these are too soft to be distinguishable by the ear as separate notes, though they have the effect of colouring the tone quality of the note which *is* heard: the fundamental note produced by the full length of the string. A string which is lightly touched at a node, however, ceases to vibrate throughout its entire length. Thus the fundamental note no longer sounds, and only the faint harmonic can be heard – distinctive in character and quite different from the sound produced by a string in the ordinary way. For special effects, composers may indicate that it is this harmonic sound which is required. The use of harmonics also makes it possible to play higher notes than could otherwise be obtained.

String harmonics are of two kinds: 'natural', those produced by touching a node of an open string, and 'artificial', those produced by touching a node of a stopped string. In notation, both may be indicated by a tiny circle written

above the note *at the pitch at which it will be heard*, e.g. – . Natural

harmonics on string instruments are sometimes thought to have a flute-like quality, and hence may be found marked *flautato* or *flautando* (after the Italian for 'flute') or 'flageolet notes' (after a now-obsolete recorder-type instrument).

A great deal of confusion arises out of the fact that it is often possible to produce a harmonic note in more than one way, and alternative systems of notation are sometimes used showing *how the note is to be produced* (basically by indicating the node to be touched) rather than the pitch at which it will be heard. This is too complicated and technical a matter to be explained in detail here, particularly as methods of notation have not always been uniform, but it should be observed that they always involve the use of a diamond-shaped note, e.g. ♩ rather than ♩ . One particular device of notation is sufficiently standardised to be worth noting: it is used to represent an artificial harmonic and consists of an ordinary note (to show how the string is to be stopped), with a diamond-shaped note a perfect 4th higher (to indicate the node to be touched). This produces a sound two octaves above the stopped note, e.g. –

(N.B. the diamond-shaped notes are always written as white notes.)

What may drive even a patient reader almost to despair is the information that, when a o is written above a note, it does not invariably indicate a harmonic. It is also used to show that an *open* string is required. Thus on the violin are to be played as the open notes of the D, A and E strings respectively, not as stopped notes on lower strings. Fortunately, the context generally prevents any misunderstanding. In printed music, furthermore, an oval-shaped 'nought' sign (as in the example above) is nowadays generally used for this purpose rather than a circle.

19/5 Vibrato

To give the sound more warmth and expressiveness, string players make liberal use of **vibrato**. The Italian word literally means 'vibrating' or 'quivering', and it implies performing a note with slight but rapid and regular variations of pitch. In string playing it is produced by rocking the finger of the left hand which is stopping the string – thus it cannot be applied to a note produced by an open string, nor to very short notes. The word itself is not normally written in the music: the use of vibrato is assumed in passages where it is appropriate, although occasionally a composer may direct *senza vibrato* where a straight sound is required.

19/6   The guitar

The **guitar** is probably the most widely-played string instrument in modern times, although it is not normally employed as an orchestral instrument. It has a long history stretching back to the medieval period and has existed in a number of different forms. The various types in general use today, however, are all quite recent developments. Obviously this is true of the electric guitar, but even instruments which are regarded as more traditional, such as the flamenco guitar and the so-called 'classical' guitar, only consolidated their present shape at the end of the 19th and the beginning of the 20th centuries. Largely under the influence of the great Spanish player, Segovia (1893–1987), and his followers, many leading composers have been inspired to write for the modern classical guitar. It is this instrument which will be considered here.

The classical guitar has six strings, normally tuned to the following written notes –

However, these notes actually *sound* an octave lower, since guitar music is always written an octave above its true pitch. Only the treble clef is used –

even for the lowest notes. A written range extending up to ⟶ can safely be assumed: higher notes are possible.

As on orchestral string instruments, notes may be played on open or on stopped strings. Vibrato may be used, and harmonics can also be produced. Bowing marks and directions such as *pizzicato, arco* and *col legno* are not applicable since a bow, of course, is not used. The guitar's lap-held position, however, makes easy some plucking techniques which are difficult or impossible to use (pizzicato) on orchestral strings, e.g. rapid reiterations of a single note. The guitar also differs from the orchestral strings in that chords are part of its staple diet: indeed, Berlioz described the instrument as 'especially an instrument of harmony'. Chords produced by thrumming the fingers across the strings are a distinctive part of its technique and the most characteristic of all its sounds.

19/7   The harp

In essence, the harp is merely a frame holding parallel strings of different lengths which are plucked by the fingers. Simple instruments with this basic construction have existed since at least 2500 B.C., but it was not until the early

19th century A.D. that the elaborate 'double-action' harp which is the modern concert instrument was developed, and only gradually during the 19th century that it became a more-or-less regular member of the orchestra (see p.232). Its music is written on two staves bracketed together, like that of the piano, and uses the treble and bass clefs.

The harp works on a quite different principle from the other string instruments already mentioned, since the length of the string allowed to vibrate is not controlled by the player's fingers. On the modern harp there are 47 strings, initially tuned with one string for each note of a scale of C♭ major, thus –

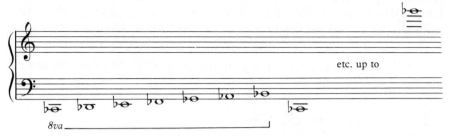

However, the strings can be stopped by means of a pedal-operated mechanism, so as to raise their pitch by either one or two semitones. There are seven pedals, each controlling *all* the strings with the same letter name – one for all the Cs, one for all the Ds, and so on. Each pedal has three positions: in one position the strings it controls are all open, e.g. C♭; in the next position they are raised a semitone, e.g. C♮; and in the next they are raised by another semitone, e.g. C♯. It is thus impossible to play, say, C♮ and C♯ simultaneously, though the effect can be produced by enharmonic substitutes, e.g. B♯ and C♯, or C♮ and D♭.

Since the player has both hands free to pluck the strings, rich patterns of notes can easily be played. Arpeggios, which in fact take their name from the instrument, are particularly well suited to it. So also are chords, though with not more than four notes in each hand as the little fingers are not used. Another very characteristic technique is the *glissando*: a rapid scale, either up or down, produced by sweeping the fingers across the strings.

Always, however, the practical problems of altering the notes with the pedals have to be allowed for. Rapid chromatic scales, for example, are not possible: nor, even at quite moderate speeds, are chordal passages which require several pedal changes between the chords. In a glissando it has to be remembered that *all* the strings between the top and bottom notes will be played, so all their tunings have to be made clear. The most usual way of doing this is to write out the first octave in full. Some composers, however, indicate the notes (or changes of notes) by giving their letter names plus accidentals.

The example below combines both methods. It is sufficient to show just the start and finish of a glissando with a guide-line between them, although *glissando* or *gliss.* may be added.

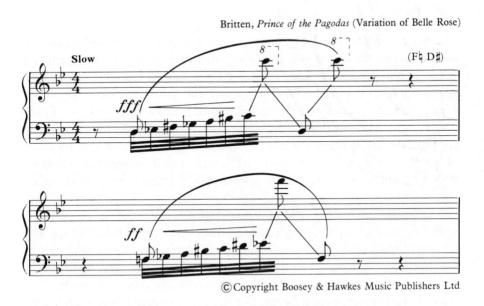

Britten, *Prince of the Pagodas* (Variation of Belle Rose)

© Copyright Boosey & Hawkes Music Publishers Ltd

(As implied by the open-ended beams, the time values of the notes at the start of a glissando are not to be taken literally: all the notes in a glissando are fitted into the time available – equivalent to a quaver for each upward and downward glissando in this example.)

Some chords can be played as glissandos, provided there are available enharmonic equivalents to make it possible for all the strings to be used. A dominant 7th in the key of A (E, G♯, B, D), for example, can be managed by setting the other notes to F♭ (= E), A♭ (= G♯) and C♭ (= B).

As on the violin etc., harmonics can be produced. They are invariably shown by the small circle symbol mentioned earlier, but in harp music this always means that the actual sound is *an octave higher* than the written note. Two directions are used for special effects: *près de la table*, meaning that the strings are to be plucked near the sound board to produce a somewhat metallic tone; and *sons étouffés*, a technique of 'damping' a string (stopping it vibrating) as soon as it has been played, thus producing a dry, staccato sound. The Italian for 'whispering', *bisbigliando*, is appropriately used to indicate a type of *tremolo*, with repeated notes played softly and quickly by the fingers of both hands.

CHAPTER 20

Woodwind and Brass instruments

The basic principle of all wind instruments can be easily demonstrated: by blowing across the edge of one end of a tube, such as a piece of metal piping, it is possible to produce a note. The same result can be obtained by blowing across the neck of a bottle. What happens is that vibrations are set up at the edge, which then cause the entire column of air enclosed by the tube to vibrate in much the same way that a string on a string instrument vibrates. The longer the tube, the longer the column of air; and, consequently, the deeper the note. Other considerations also affect the pitch of the note: for example, how hard it is blown, and whether the tube is open or closed (as in a bottle) at the other end.

The tone quality of the note (whether it sounds like a flute or an oboe, for instance) depends upon many considerations, such as the tube's shape and what it is made of; but the most important is what causes the air to vibrate in the first place. Blowing across the edge of a tube is only one way. Another is to direct the breath against a reed set into the end of the tube. Yet another is to buzz the lips against a separate mouthpiece made of metal, also inserted into the tubing.

Wind instruments are traditionally divided into two broad categories: **woodwind** and **brass**. Neither term is really satisfactory today. The so-called 'woodwind' instruments are often made from materials other than wood, including metal; and although modern 'brass' instruments are always made from metal of *some* kind, the metal is not necessarily brass. The unsuitability of the names by which they are known does not mean, however, that the two categories are no longer valid. Wind instruments can still be usefully classified in two groups, but according to the way they work rather than the materials they are made of.

In woodwind instruments the sound is produced in one of two ways: (1) by blowing across some kind of edge made in the instrument itself, producing what are called 'edge tones' (this group includes flutes, recorders and whistles of all kinds); or (2) by means of a reed (as in oboes, clarinets and saxophones). In brass instruments (trumpets, trombones, tubas etc.) the sound is produced by the vibrations of the lips against a mouthpiece. Woodwind instruments are fixed in length (except for slight adjustments made in tuning); while brass instruments (except those of the simplest kind, such as bugles) can be varied in length by means of slides, valves and other devices.

20/1 Woodwind: flue instruments

20/1a Recorders

Instruments whose sounds are created as edge tones are described as 'flue' instruments. One of the simplest in design is the **recorder** (or *Blockflöte* in German). It is also one of the most familiar, since most people have experimented with one when they were young – or if not a recorder then a tin whistle (or penny whistle), which works on the same principle. One should not, however, think of the recorder as a mere toy. It was in regular use until Handel's time – much of his 'flute' music was in fact written for what we should call a recorder – and many composers have written for it since it was revived in the 20th century.

The recorder consists of a tube of wood or ivory or, in modern mass-produced instruments, of plastic. When the player blows into it, the breath is channelled against a lip (or 'fipple') cut into the head joint which forms part of the instrument. (Even a complete beginner can be sure of producing a note at the first attempt, which is more than can be said of most other wind instruments!) Holes which the player can cover with the fingers are set in line along the length of the tube on its upper surface, with one underneath for the thumb. When all are closed, the instrument produces its lowest note, because the air then vibrates through the entire length of the tube. If the hole at the far end is opened, however, the tube is in effect shortened, since the air vibrates only as far as the open hole; thus the resulting note is higher. Opening the next hole as well makes the note higher still, and so on until all the holes are opened. Further notes can be produced by more complicated combinations of open and closed holes, and by increased blowing pressure.

In the past, recorders were made in many different sizes. Nowadays, four are in general use, by far the most common being the descant recorder (= soprano recorder in the U.S.A.). Their lowest-sounding notes are –

| **Descant** | **Treble** | **Tenor** | **Bass** |
| (or Soprano) | (or Alto) | | |

For the sake of convenience, however, music for the descant and bass recorders is normally written an octave *lower* than it sounds. To show this, a tiny 8 is sometimes written above the clefs they use: and respectively. All instruments except the bass can expect to have a range of two octaves plus a tone. On most bass instruments the highest notes are unobtainable, and a more practicable limit would be an octave plus a major 6th.

20/1b The flute family

The **flute** works in much the same way as the recorder but with two modifications. First, the player holds the instrument sideways and produces the sound by blowing across the edge of a hole in its side. The player has to find exactly the right angle which will produce a sound: the breath is not aimed automatically by the instrument itself, as it is in recorders and whistles. Secondly, the system of holes controlling the vibrations in the air column is more elaborate, necessitating a mechanism of finger keys, levers and padded hole covers. The system used today is still known as the 'Boehm system', after Theobald Boehm who invented it in the middle of the 19th century, although some improvements have subsequently been incorporated. The flute's lowest note is normally middle C (some instruments can produce the B below), and the range extends to the C three octaves above, or even D.

Because it is played sideways, the modern flute may be described as a 'transverse flute'. The baroque predecessor of the modern instrument was known by the Italian term *flauto traverso* or, in Britain, as the 'German flute'. The word *flauto* by itself at that period generally implied the recorder; it was also known by the French term *flûte à bec* or as the 'English flute'.

A smaller version of the flute is the **piccolo**, which literally means 'small' in Italian. Being smaller, its sounds are of course higher; consequently, the fingering required to produce a particular note on the flute will produce a higher note when applied to the piccolo. The piccolo is in fact designed to sound exactly one octave higher than the flute. Thus the fingering which on the flute would produce

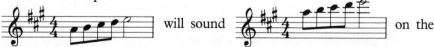

piccolo. Since the fingerings remain the same, it is easier for the players if the written notes remain the same too, so piccolo music is written not at the pitch it actually sounds but an octave lower. (Putting it the other way round, music played on the piccolo sounds an octave higher than written.) In one detail the piccolo does not correspond with the flute: its lowest note is D.

There is also a larger flute, though it is not very common. It goes under various names: **alto flute** (the most usual term) or 'bass flute' or 'flute in G'. Again the fingering is the same as for the ordinary flute, but being larger it produces lower notes. In the case of the alto flute, the notes are a perfect 4th higher than it sounds, e.g. the written notes

alto flute. Notice that the key signature has been altered accordingly.

20/2   Transposing instruments

At this stage, some general comments are needed about instruments whose sounding notes are different from their written notes. They are called **transposing instruments**. Several have already been mentioned – double bass, guitar, descant and bass recorders, piccolo, alto flute – but there are more to come. As has been explained, transposition is used for one or both of two reasons: (1) to avoid many ledger lines, (2) to keep the same written notes for the same fingerings when the player uses different-sized versions of the same instrument. It is thus a practical and sensible system, even though it may seem perverse to musicians such as pianists who are not faced with the problems of playing alternative versions of their instrument.

Difficulties may easily arise if the terms applying to transposition are not properly understood and used. Transposing instruments are described by the note which is sounded when C is played: an instrument 'in B♭', for example, is so called because it sounds B♭ when the written note C is played. Similarly, an instrument 'in F' sounds F when written C is played. If in rehearsal one wishes to refer to a certain note in the music, it is important to make it clear whether the written note or the sounding note is meant. The sounding note is called the 'concert' note: thus, on a B♭ instrument, 'written C' is the same as 'concert B♭' (or 'B♭ concert'), and 'written G' is the same as 'F concert' (or 'concert F').

20/3   Woodwind: reeds

Like the flute and the piccolo, other instruments may be made in different sizes, e.g. these three groups of related instruments:

1) oboe, cor anglais (French for English horn), bassoon, double bassoon;
2) clarinets in various keys, bass clarinet;
3) saxophones in various keys.

All of these have two things in common. First, like the flute and piccolo, they are essentially tubes with holes which are opened and closed by means of a mechanism of keys, levers and padded hole-covers. Secondly, in all of them the air in the tube is made to vibrate by the player 'tonguing'[1] a piece of reed set in the end of the instrument. Actually, the reed in the oboe, cor anglais, bassoon and double bassoon is made of *two* pieces of cane bound together: all these are therefore 'double-reed' instruments. The clarinets and saxophones, on the other hand, are 'single-reed' instruments.

[1] See 20/6.

20/3a Double reeds: oboe, cor anglais, bassoon, double bassoon

The table below deals with the double-reed instruments. It shows their bottom notes and also their approximate upper limits, but it must be emphasised that how high a performer can play often depends upon individual skill. Skill may affect the lowest notes as well: the lowest 'possible' notes are not always easy to produce (although they are actually *easier* in instruments of the clarinet family). The table also shows the clefs that the instruments use: the bassoon, for example, uses the bass and tenor clefs but not the treble clef (it rarely ventures so high that this would be an advantage). On the right-hand side, transpositions are given where necessary – the **oboe** and **bassoon** are not transposing instruments but the **cor anglais** and **double bassoon** are. The cor anglais, it will be seen, sounds a perfect 5th *lower* than its written notes; therefore its music must be transposed a perfect 5th *higher* than the required sounds, and the key signature revised accordingly. Thus, if the key actually heard is F major, the cor anglais part will be written a 5th higher in C major; if the key is E minor, the cor anglais part will be written in B minor, and so on.

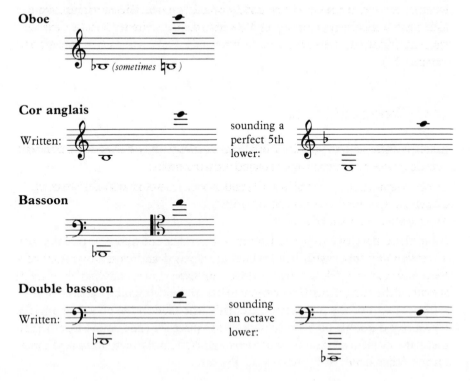

20/3b Single reeds: clarinets and saxophones

The next table below gives the corresponding information for members of the **clarinet** family. The B♭ instrument is by far the most commonly used today, followed by the one in A. The E♭ instrument and the bass clarinet in B♭ may also be encountered. Clarinets in other keys have been made in the past, but now they are rare or obsolete[1]: parts written for them are generally transposed and played on one of the instruments listed below. Another rarity in our own times is the **basset horn**: a type of alto clarinet pitched in F (sounding a 5th lower than written), much favoured by Mozart.

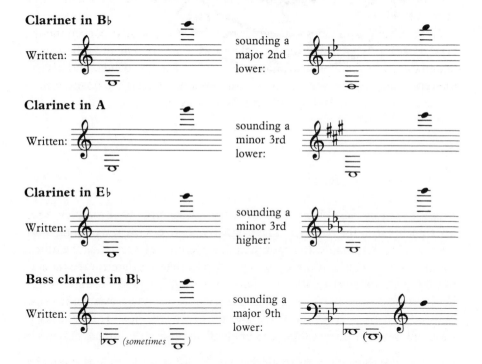

Clarinet in B♭

Written: sounding a major 2nd lower:

Clarinet in A

Written: sounding a minor 3rd lower:

Clarinet in E♭

Written: sounding a minor 3rd higher:

Bass clarinet in B♭

Written: (sometimes)   sounding a major 9th lower:

A **bass clarinet** may be written in two different systems; either (as above) in the 'French' system, or in the 'German' system where the notes are written a major 2nd higher than they sound, in either the treble or bass clef.

---

[1]A modern clarinet in C (i.e. a non-transposing instrument) has, however, been produced, with features which make it suitable for young players – notably the size of its tone holes, the stretch of its keys and its light weight.

The **saxophone** was invented in about 1840 by Adolphe Sax. The instrument is made in many different sizes, but those most generally used today are the B♭ soprano, the E♭ alto, the B♭ tenor and the E♭ baritone. They all have the same written range –

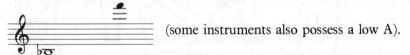 (some instruments also possess a low A).

All are written in the treble clef. All are transposing instruments: the B♭ soprano sounds a tone lower than written, the E♭ alto a major 6th lower, the B♭ tenor an octave plus a tone lower, and the E♭ baritone an octave plus a major 6th lower.

None of the saxophones is a regular member of the orchestra, even though very occasionally one may be brought in as a soloist. On the other hand, saxophones are familiar instruments in jazz and dance bands, and also in military bands; moreover, an increasing amount of music is being written especially for them, playing both as soloists and in groups.

20/4 Brass

20/4a The harmonic series

From a purely scientific point of view, there are even simpler wind instruments than the recorder. The **bugle** is one. In essence it is nothing more than a length of tubing with a mouthpiece at the end. It is true that the tube is wound round to make it more manageable and that it is flared at the far end, but there are no holes or other mechanisms to regulate the air column within it. Nevertheless, the player is not restricted to just one note; several others can be produced by varying the shape and tension of the lips. Theoretically at least, any piece of metal tubing can be made to produce a number of notes in this way. For example, a tube which has 𝄢 as its lowest possible note can be made to sound a whole series of notes, called the harmonic series. Here are the first 16 –

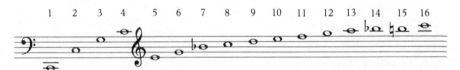

The lowest possible note is the 'fundamental' or 'pedal note', the note above it (an octave higher) is the 'second harmonic', the next note the 'third harmonic' and so on. Harmonics are also called 'partials', the fundamental note being the 'first partial': 2–16 are 'upper partials' or 'overtones'.

In practice, no instrument can produce all the notes of the harmonic series. Other considerations apart from the player's skill affect what is practicable: for example, the size of the cavity in the tubing (= its 'bore'). Even the fundamental itself cannot always be made to sound. A bugle, for instance, can sound the 2nd to 6th harmonics, so it has five available notes. Another limitation is that some harmonics (the 7th, 11th, 13th and 14th) are out of tune when compared with the notes produced by equal temperament (see the footnote on p.23 in Part I).

20/4b Slide instruments: trombones

Tubes of different length will of course have different fundamental notes, and therefore the notes of their harmonic series will be different. For example, a tube with D as its fundamental note will produce this harmonic series –

Instruments which can vary the length of the tubing can therefore not only change their fundamental notes but also produce a different harmonic series from each. The most obvious example of an instrument with variable-length tubing is the **trombone,** since it is easy to see the tube being made longer or shorter as the slide is pushed out or pulled in. (One piece of tubing slides in and out of another like a telescope.) As the slide is extended, the tube gets longer and the sound becomes lower. The player must judge just how far to extend the slide in order to move from one note to the next. Actually, seven positions are used, a semitone apart: in the first position the tube is at its shortest length, and in the seventh at its longest.

Trombones exist in various sizes, but the most common is the **tenor trombone,** also called the 'Bb trombone' or 'Bb tenor trombone'. Its music is written in the bass and tenor clefs; and in spite of being called a 'Bb' trombone, it is treated as a *non-transposing* instrument, i.e. its notes sound as written.[1] The table on the next page shows its seven fundamental notes and, above them, the harmonic series (as far as the eighth harmonic) derived from each:

---

[1] In brass bands, however, the trombone *is* treated as a transposing instrument: its part is written a major 9th higher than it sounds, and in the *treble* clef.

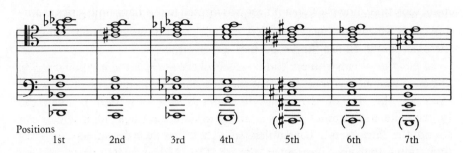

Positions
    1st   2nd   3rd   4th   5th   6th   7th

Expert players can produce higher harmonics. The fundamental notes themselves are more doubtful: those in the first three or four positions (B♭ to A♭ or G) are occasionally used, but for practical purposes 𝄢 can be regarded as the bottom note.

A lower version of the same instrument is the **bass trombone**. This has never been as standardised as the tenor trombone, and the term has been used to describe several slightly different instruments. Here we need mention only two: the bass trombone in G and the tenor-bass trombone. The bass trombone in G lies a minor 3rd lower than the tenor trombone, with 𝄢 as the lowest note (apart from the fundamentals). It is still sometimes used in bands but has largely been replaced by the tenor-bass trombone. Although the tenor-bass trombone is designed to go down as far as B or (with some refinements) even lower, it would be prudent to regard 𝄢 as the practicable limit. Whatever type of bass trombone is used, it is treated as a non-transposing instrument with its music written in the bass clef.

20/4c Crooks and valves: horns, trumpets etc.

Extending a metal tube by means of a slide mechanism is a very old principle, and trombones are among the oldest instruments in the modern orchestra: in their essential design they have remained virtually unchanged since the late 15th century. Another way of lengthening a tube, which was once very common but which has now been superseded completely, consisted of inserting an additional length of tubing called a **crook** at the mouthpiece end. With the addition of a crook the tube became longer and its fundamental note lower; thus the notes of its harmonic series were lowered too. Trumpets and horns used to employ crooks, and players had to have several of them in order to be able to produce whatever harmonic series might be required. Changing a crook took time, however, so a player was limited to one harmonic series at any given moment in the music. Naturally, composers specified the crook which would produce the most useful notes. If the music were in E♭, for example, an E♭ crook would most probably be chosen, giving the series –

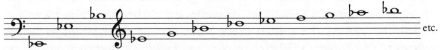

But these notes would be of little value if the music were in D major: a D crook would be more likely to be used instead (producing the notes already shown on p.213) or possibly an A crook –

Horns and trumpets continued to use crooks until well into the 19th century. Their music was always written in notes derived from the series on C (see p.212), and without a key signature, regardless of the crooks actually being used. During the 19th century, however, crooks were gradually discarded in favour of the modern system of **valves**. Valves (also called 'pistons') are used to open up or close off loops in the tubing, thus varying its overall length. At the mere press of a valve the fundamental note can be changed, together with its harmonic series. Different combinations of valves bring different lengths of tubing into operation, and by these means it became possible to produce all the notes of the chromatic scale.

Not only trumpets and horns use valves: so do many other brass instruments, most of which are used in bands rather than in orchestras. (The terms 'band' and 'orchestra' will be discussed in more detail in Chapter 22.) The standard orchestral instruments which use valves are –

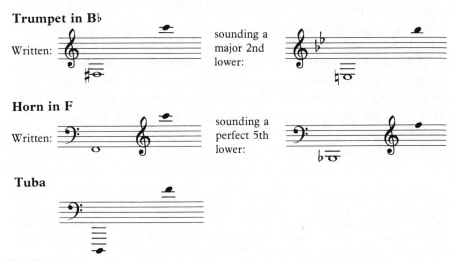

The Bb **trumpet** is the most common, but orchestral music sometimes includes trumpet parts written in C (sounding as written) or in other keys, e.g. A (sounding a minor 3rd lower), D (sounding a tone higher), Eb or E (sounding a minor or major 3rd higher). In orchestral music it is now quite common for trumpets to use key signatures, e.g. if the music is in F major, a Bb trumpet part will be written a tone higher in G major, with F♯ as the key signature. Old habits die hard, however, and much 20th-century music is to be found where the trumpet parts are written without a key signature, accidentals being added as and when necessary.

An instrument resembling the trumpet is the **cornet**, and it has the same range. Although a rarity in the orchestra it is a standard instrument in bands, where both Bb and Eb instruments are used. The Eb instrument sounds a minor 3rd above the written notes. It is also known as a 'soprano cornet'.

The **horn** (or 'French horn' as it is often called) uses treble and bass clefs. When the treble clef is used (which is most of the time), the music is written a perfect 5th higher than it sounds.[1] That having been said, we arrive in an area of some confusion. First of all, music in the bass clef used always to be written a perfect 4th lower than it sounds. Although the modern convention (shown above) is to treat the bass clef like the treble clef and write its music a 5th above, the old notation may still be encountered. Secondly, it used to be the invariable custom to write horn music without a key signature, adding accidentals as required. Quite early in the 20th century, however, some composers began to use key signatures for horns. Elgar, for example, wrote without them in the 'Enigma' Variations (1898–9) but with them in the Cello Concerto (1919). But again the old practice has persisted, and in this case more strongly. Sometimes the two methods exist side by side: even in the same work one may find passages where key signatures are not used for the horns, and others where they are.

For a long time the **tuba** in F was the recognised orchestral instrument, but it has been largely replaced by the tuba in Eb and, more recently, the tuba in C; and the tuba in Bb (or 'double Bb') is sometimes employed. Whichever instrument is used, the part is written in the bass clef at concert pitch. Brass band players use the Eb and Bb tubas (they normally refer to the tuba as 'bass'), but the parts are written in the treble clef, the Eb instrument being transposed a major 13th higher than the sound, and the Bb instrument two octaves plus a tone higher.

---

[1] Although this is the standard notation, a few composers continued to notate their horn music as though for crooked horns long after the latter had disappeared. As late as 1948, for example, Richard Strauss wrote for horns in F, Eb and D in his *Four Last Songs*, knowing perfectly well that in fact only the modern F horns would be used. Incidentally, in the same work he treated the trumpets similarly, writing their parts without key signatures in F, Eb, D and C.

The tuba is but one member of a group of related instruments, mainly used in bands, including: the **flugelhorn** (or soprano saxhorn[1]), primarily a band instrument written in the treble clef and sounding a major 2nd lower; the **E♭ horn** (or alto saxhorn), written in the treble clef and sounding a major 6th lower; the **baritone** (a tenor tuba or B♭ saxhorn), another band instrument written in the treble clef a 9th higher than the sound; and the **euphonium** (a tenor tuba) – a heavier-sounding instrument than the baritone due to its wider bore – but notated in the same way. (In orchestral music the tenor tuba/euphonium is sometimes written a tone higher in the bass clef.)

20/5 Mutes in wind instruments

Sounds produced by brass instruments can be not only softened but also changed in tone quality by the insertion of a pear- or cone-shaped mute made of metal, wood, cardboard etc. into the bell (the widening of the tube at the end where the sound comes out). The standard directions are *con sord.* and *senza sord.* as in string music (see p.200). To create a wider range of effects, jazz musicians pioneered many other kinds of mute (e.g. the *wa-wa* mute), some of which are placed over or near the bell. Even a bowler hat has been used in this way.

Horn players have an additional way of muting: by inserting the right hand into the bell. Partial insertion of the hand has always been a method of adjusting the *pitch* of notes: indeed, before the invention of valves, players relied heavily on this method to produce notes otherwise unobtainable (the old crooked or 'natural' horns are also called 'hand' horns). However, not only the pitch but also the tone is affected; and the characteristic, muted quality of notes 'stopped' when the hand is fully inserted is a sound frequently exploited in valve horns. Notes to be played in this way are shown by a little + over them plus, possibly, the word 'stopped' (or its French, German or Italian equivalents: *sons bouchés*, *gestopft* or *chiuso*). A tiny ° over the note then indicates that it is to be played in the normal way, as an open note. Forcing the breath produces a brassy sound (*cuivré* in French) which adds extra colour to stopped notes, though the technique can be applied to open notes as well.

Woodwind instruments use no special devices as mutes: in fact they are almost never muted. When, as very exceptionally happens, the direction *con sord.* is given to an instrument such as the oboe or saxophone, the player merely stuffs a handkerchief into the bell.

---

[1]Named after Adolphe Sax, who also invented the saxophone.

20/6 Tonguing

The tongue is vital in the playing of wind instruments. It functions as a kind of valve in controlling the flow of air from the lungs. To stop the air it is placed in a forward position: behind the teeth (against the palate) for flue and brass instruments, or pressed lightly against the reed in the case of reed instruments. When it is drawn sharply back (as in saying the consonant 't'), the pressure of air is released and vibrations are started by the reed or in one of the other ways described earlier. If each individual note is started in this way, the notes are said to be separately 'tongued'; and if there are no slurs or other signs to the contrary, it must be assumed that this is what is required. The addition of staccato dots over notes shows that they are to be tongued particularly crisply.

Once the breath has been released and the sound started, it may be possible to play a succession of notes without the tongue interrupting the supply of breath. The result is an extremely smooth legato, and a group of notes played thus is marked by a slur. But a legato effect can also be obtained by the use of a less explosive consonant than 't' to start the sound, such as 'd' or 'dh'. 'Legato tonguing' implies individually tongued notes but played as smoothly as possible. Here it has to be added that tonguing techniques vary according to the nature of the instrument. Legato tonguing, for example, is common with brass instruments because a completely slurred legato would often be impracticable, if not impossible.

When notes are to be tongued separately but very rapidly (e.g. in semiquaver passages at fast speeds), more elaborate methods of tonguing are needed. A succession of notes produced by the tip of the tongue – 'tttttt' etc. – would soon become tiring, so a 'k' sound produced with the back of the tongue is used in alternation: 'tktktk' etc. (double tonguing) or, in groups of three, 'tkttkt' etc. (triple tonguing). Double and triple tonguing also make it possible for very rapid repetitions of a single note to be performed.

An unusual kind of tonguing, occasionally required by 20th-century composers, is created by rolling an 'r' on the tip of the tongue. This technique, known as 'flutter-tonguing', is generally indicated by the use of tremolo signs (e.g. ♪) and/or in words: the German *Flatterzunge* (abbreviated as *Flzg.*) is often used. Flutter-tonguing is particularly suited to flue instruments such as the flute, but it can be successful on others too, such as the trumpet and trombone.

CHAPTER 21

Percussion and Keyboard instruments

Percussion instruments are instruments which are struck or shaken. Some produce notes of definite pitch; others a mere crash, thud, rattle etc. – sounds of indefinite pitch. Throughout the world there are very many different types, and often different ways of playing instruments of the same type. By no means all have found their way into Western music, though the modern orchestra has used an increasingly wide variety. Here we can describe only the more common ones. It will be convenient if they are divided into those which produce notes of (a) definite pitch and (b) indefinite pitch –

(a) timpani, xylophone, glockenspiel, vibraphone, tubular bells;

(b) bass drum, side drum, cymbals, gong (tam-tam), triangle, tambourine.

21/1 Pitched percussion

21/1a Timpani

By far the most important percussion instruments in the orchestra are the kettle-drums or **timpani** (usually called 'timps' in ordinary conversation). Until the early 19th century they were the only percussion instruments used in orchestras, with very occasional exceptions where special effects were needed (e.g. in opera). Even after that they remained the most frequently used of the percussion instruments, and many works employ no other.

They are virtually never used singly. Normally at least two (in different sizes) are required; often three, four or even more. They are made of copper and shaped like a large basin or witch's cauldron, with a skin tightly stretched across the top which the player beats with padded sticks. The tension of the skin, and thus the pitch of the note, is adjusted by screw-taps around the rim. Modern drums, however, more usually have a pedal mechanism instead. This produces the same result, but more quickly and conveniently. It also makes possible a sliding effect from one note to another (*glissando*).

Each drum has a range of a perfect 5th or slightly more. They are tuned with some overlapping, but between them a set of two would have a range of

, and a set of three . Smaller

and larger drums can add a note or two either side, but they are rare. Some composers now use key signatures for their timpani parts, but the traditional procedure was to write without key signatures or accidentals, the required tunings being specified at the beginning (see p.234). Directions such as *muta A in Bb* (Italian for 'change A to Bb') indicate changes of tuning during the course of the music. A drum 'roll' (alternating drum-strokes played as quickly as possible on one drum, giving the effect of a continuous sound) is written thus –

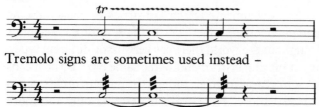

Tremolo signs are sometimes used instead –

but they are less satisfactory since, unless enough diagonal lines are used, they could be taken to mean an exact number of reiterated notes (see p.99 in Part I).

21/1b Tuned bars and tubes

The **xylophone** has wooden bars laid out in two rows like piano keys, and tuned in the same way. They are normally struck by wooden sticks with small egg-shaped heads, and produce a bright, dry tone quality. Modern orchestral instruments have a hollow tube (a 'resonator') underneath each bar, in which the sound vibrations are reinforced. Both the **vibraphone** and the **glockenspiel** have bars similarly arranged like piano keys, but made of metal. The vibraphone also has a resonator tube under each bar, with a disc in the end of each tube which is made to spin by a motor, producing a pulsating effect. Its sound is much creamier and more sustained than that of the glockenspiel, whose notes have a silvery quality like that of small bells, but the tone of both can be modified by using different kinds of sticks.

The vibraphone sounds at its written pitch, the xylophone an octave higher, and the glockenspiel two octaves higher. All three instrumemts are notated in the treble clef, but it would be misleading to specify a compass for any of them since instruments of varying ranges are made.

Tubular bells (or 'orchestral chimes') are a series of metal tubes hanging in a frame. The player uses a wooden mallet to strike the top of the tube. The notes are written in the treble clef, usually from middle C to F on the top line.

21/2 Unpitched percussion

The indefinite-pitch instruments naturally do not need a five-line stave, still less a clef or a key signature. Often their parts are written on single lines. Nevertheless, an ordinary stave *is* sometimes used, with each instrument allocated a particular line or space, and possibly even a treble or bass clef as well. This can make it much easier to spot which instrument is which, particularly when one player is dealing with more than one instrument.

21/2a Bass drum and side drum

In a band on the march the **bass drum** is supported on the player's chest. It is a large drum with a skin on either side: one played with the left hand and one with the right. Elsewhere, the bass drum may rest on a stand or on the floor. When used in dance bands and similar groups, it is usually played by a single drum stick operated by a pedal. Orchestral bass drums vary considerably in size; moreover in the orchestra a single-headed bass drum (called a 'gong drum') is sometimes used instead of the double-headed version. Bass drum sticks have a large knob of felt at the end, though other types may be used for special effects. The **side drum** is similar in shape to the conventional bass drum, but much smaller, and it is played with the skins at the top and bottom, not at the sides. It gets its name from the fact that, when it is carried, it is positioned slightly to the player's side, but in the orchestra it rests on a stand. Stretched across the surface of the skin underneath are strips made of wire or gut. They are called 'snares': the side drum is also known as a 'snare drum'. Wooden sticks are used, producing a hard, bright tone to which the snares add a rattling quality. If the rattle is not wanted, the snares can be unfastened – the music is marked 'without snares' or, in Italian, *scordato* or *senza corda*.

Very intricate rhythmic patterns are possible on the side drum, and it has several characteristic two-stick drum strokes (such as the 'flam' and the 'drag') which are notated by grace notes –

The *tr* sign indicates a roll, as on the timpani. Like the timpani, both the side drum and the bass drum rolls are sometimes written with tremolo signs instead of *tr* signs, but the latter are safer for the reason already explained.

21/2b The tambourine

The **tambourine** is a small, hand-held drum with a single skin. It has narrow wooden sides in which are set pairs of brass discs called 'jingles'. There are various ways of playing it:

1) It can be struck with the player's fist, knuckles or finger-tips, or it can be banged against the knee.

2) It can be shaken so that only the jingles sound; this is the equivalent of a drum roll and can be notated in the same way.

3) A moistened thumb can be rubbed round the edge of the skin, causing the jingles to vibrate in a 'jingle roll'. The two types of roll can be marked 'shake' or 'thumb' to distinguish them.

21/2c Cymbal, gong and triangle

A **cymbal** is a large circular plate of thin metal with a strap or other holding device at the centre. It can be suspended and struck with a stick; with two sticks a roll (notated like drum rolls) is possible. Two cymbals can be clashed together or gently slid past each other. The direction *laissez vibrer* is the standard way of showing that the cymbals are to be allowed to continue to vibrate until the sound dies away naturally; *sec* means that the sound is to be damped immediately, usually by pressing the cymbals against the player's body. (Both terms are French.) Jazz bands use a variety of cymbals, the most familiar of which is the 'hi-hat' – a pair of cymbals mounted on a stand and clashed against each other by means of a pedal mechanism, though they are also played with sticks or wire brushes.

The **gong** is similar to the cymbal except that it is heavier, has a deep rim, and is normally played with a heavily padded beater. The particular type of gong normally used in the orchestra is a large one called a **tam-tam**.

Another metal instrument is the **triangle**: a steel bar, shaped as its name implies, and struck with a small steel rod. Its equivalent of a roll (and notated in the same ways) is achieved by moving the rod rapidly from one side to another inside the instrument.

21/3 Keyboard instruments

21/3a The celesta

A keyboard is in itself nothing more than a mechanical device: a means of operating other mechanisms which then cause sounds to be made. Its simplest application is in the **celesta**, in which the keyboard controls a series of hammers which strike against metal bars. Thence it can be regarded as a kind of keyboard glockenspiel, and its sound is somewhat similar though softer. The celesta can add an indispensable colour to the orchestra, as in the 'Dance of the Sugar-Plum Fairy' in Tchaikovsky's *The Nutcracker*. Even as an orchestral instrument, however, it is a rarity. Its music is written on two staves in the treble and bass clefs, like that of the piano, and it has a four-octave range with

$\begin{array}{c}\text{𝄢}\ \ \bo\end{array}$ as its lowest written note, but it sounds an octave higher.

With the exception of the celesta, keyboard instruments generally produce their sounds from strings, either plucked or struck, or by means of wind passing through pipes. In modern times, however, a new and increasingly popular category has been added: instruments whose sounds are electronically generated.

21/3b The piano and its precursors

The **piano** was invented early in the 18th century and by the end of that century had almost completely superseded two earlier instruments, the **harpsichord** and the **clavichord** (though these have since been revived for the performance of music originally written for them, and this has led some modern composers to write for them too). Basically, all three instruments can be thought of as having a separate string for each note of the chromatic scale, i.e. one for each note on the keyboard although, as will be seen, the matter can be a little more complicated than that.

Where the three differ in principle is in the means by which their sounds are produced. In the harpsichord, each string has a plectrum (a piece of quill or leather or, in modern instruments, plastic) by means of which it is plucked. The resulting sound is short-lived, and the player has virtually no control over its loudness. However, harpsichords often have two or more sets of strings, contrasted in tone-quality and/or pitch (e.g. one set sounding an octave higher). These may be played independently – usually there is a second keyboard (or 'manual') to make this easier – or coupled together so that they sound simultaneously. The **virginal** (or 'virginals') was a type of small, one-manual harpsichord, as was the **spinet**. What, if anything, distinguishes the two has always been a matter for debate. Regrettably, the word 'spinet' was later also applied to certain types of piano.

The **clavichord** is a much quieter instrument, intended for use in the home rather than in public places such as concert halls and churches. When a key is pressed, a thin blade of metal (a 'tangent') strikes the string. The player can control with the finger the force with which the string is struck, so that some control is exercised over the loudness of the note. To a very small extent even the pitch can be modified, since the tangent remains in contact with the string while the key is down: increased pressure can therefore alter the tension. Thus, by moving the finger up and down a vibrato is possible – an effect obtainable on a string instrument (see 19/5) but not on the piano or harpsichord. The clavichord vibrato – generally known by its German name, *Bebung* – is notated by slurred dots over the note to which it is applied,

e.g. ♩ .

In the piano the strings are again struck, but this time by padded hammers. The strings themselves may be laid out vertically (in the 'upright' piano) or horizontally (in the 'grand' piano). Low notes are produced by single strings, but the middle notes each have two strings tuned to the same pitch, and the high notes have three. After the hammer has struck the string or strings it immediately falls back, leaving the string free to vibrate until a damper silences it when the key is raised. As in the clavichord, the force with which the string is struck affects the volume of the sound: indeed, the new instrument took its full name, *pianoforte*, from its capacity to play both softly and loudly.

Another way of varying the sound is altering the position of the hammers and strings in relation to each other. A grand piano's left pedal moves the keyboard and the hammers very slightly to the right, with the result that, when a note has more than one string, one of them is not struck. This is the reason why the left pedal, popularly called the 'soft' pedal, came to be called the *una corda* (one string) pedal. The direction *una corda* (or – very rarely used – *due corde*[1], meaning 'two strings') therefore indicates that the left pedal is to be depressed; while *tre corde* (three strings) means that it is to be released again. These terms apply to upright pianos too, although here the mechanics are different: when the left pedal is pressed, the hammers are moved closer to the strings which are therefore struck less forcefully. On all pianos the right pedal, known as the 'damper' pedal (sometimes called the 'sustaining' pedal or – misleadingly – the 'loud' pedal), causes *all* the dampers to be lifted from the strings so that they continue to sound even after the keys have been released. But there is more to it than that: since all the strings are free to vibrate, even those which have not been struck vibrate very slightly in sympathy with those which have, and thus the overall sound is enriched.

Directions showing where the damper pedal is to be pressed and released are given beneath the lower stave in piano music; they can be shown in any of the following ways –

It is also possible to release and re-press the damper pedal at the half-way point, so that some of the vibrations from the notes in the previously-pedalled passage can be retained in the subsequent passage. This is known as 'half-pedalling' and can be indicated by breaks in an extended pedal line –

Con ped. and *col ped.* (both meaning 'with the pedal') are general instructions indicating that the damper pedal is to be used but leaving it to the performer to decide exactly where. Incidentally, an absence of pedal marks cannot be

[1] Some early pianos enabled the performer to choose between one, two or three strings, so there was a real difference between the directions *una corda* and *due corde* (Beethoven, for example, sometimes distinguishes between them), but this choice is not available on modern pianos.

assumed to mean that the pedal should *not* be used; the direction *senza ped.* ('without pedal'), however, is unambiguous.

Some pianos have a third pedal, situated between the other two. It is called the 'sostenuto' pedal and can be shown in the music as 'SP' or 'P3'. Its effect is to sustain notes already sounding at the moment it is pressed down but not any which are subsequently played while it is still in operation. Upright pianos sometimes have a third pedal with a quite different function: it muffles all the strings with a strip of felt, and thus deadens the sound. This is of no musical value, but it can make practising less irritating to neighbours.

Music for harpsichord, clavichord and piano is normally written on two staves; but sometimes a third stave is used for the piano, if this helps to clarify the texture of elaborate music, or the way in which it is to be played.

None of the instruments in this group is, or ever has been, completely standardised in its range. A modern concert piano generally extends from

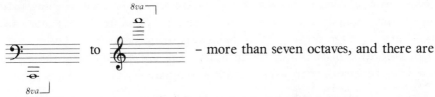

some which can go even lower; on the other hand, domestic pianos may have fewer notes. Earlier instruments were much more limited. Mozart, for

example, always wrote for a five-octave piano ranging from

. So did Beethoven in his earlier works, though by the end of his life he was writing for a six-and-a-half-octave instrument. Some harpsichords and clavichords had a range as wide as Mozart's piano, but they would have been regarded as very large in their day, particularly the clavichord.

Foreign terms for keyboard instruments have caused much confusion and misunderstanding. It is worth noting that *clavier* – originally a French word meaning simply 'keyboard' – was adopted by German-speaking composers as a term for keyboard instruments in general. (Later, they spelt it with a 'k': *Klavier*.) J. S. Bach's *Clavier-Übung* ('Keyboard Practice'), for instance, included not only pieces which could be played on a clavichord or on a harpsichord but also pieces intended for the organ. Similarly, *Das Wohltemperirte Clavier* (the original title of his '48 Preludes and Fugues'), does not refer to any particular keyboard instrument, and should therefore not be translated as 'The Well-tempered Clavichord'! Beethoven's *'Hammerklavier'* is a 'hammer-keyboard' – i.e. a piano. Other words which may be encountered are *cembalo* or *clavicembalo* (Italian) and *clavecin* (French), all referring specifically to the harpsichord. German, too, uses the Italian word *cembalo* for harpsichord, or the native word *Kielflügel*. *Flügel* now means a grand piano in German, but at an earlier period it was yet another word for the harpsichord (the word literally means 'wing' and refers to the shape).

21/3c The organ

The pipe **organ** traditionally found in churches and sometimes in concert halls, is essentially a wind instrument, but an extremely elaborate one: indeed the most elaborate of all instruments. It takes up a huge amount of space, and most of its works – bellows, wind-chests, rows of pipes, connecting rods etc. – are concealed from public view. The part which controls it all, the part the organist actually plays, is called the 'console', and the most immediately striking thing about that is that it has several manuals. Single-manual organs do exist, but they are uncommon: two manuals are the normal minimum, three are also common, and four or even more are used in very large organs. There is also the equivalent of another manual, a pedal-board, played with the feet. Its notes are arranged the same way as on a keyboard. The usual compass of manuals in modern organs is

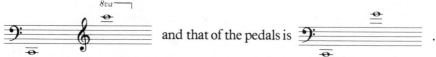

and that of the pedals is

The sign ∧ above or below a pedal note shows that it is to be played with the toe; ∪ or ○ indicates the heel. Placed above the stave these signs refer to the right foot; below it to the left.

Each manual, and also the pedal-board, controls sets of pipes. A single set or 'rank' of pipes includes a separate pipe for each note on the keyboard; it is known as a 'stop' after the draw-stop on the console which brings the pipes into action when it is pulled out. The draw-stops are arranged vertically on each side of the manuals. Modern organs often use stop-keys instead: these are set out horizontally above the manuals and make an electrical contact when they are pressed down. Any number of stops can be played simultaneously, and the stops on different manuals can be played together when the manuals are coupled. Similarly, the pedals can be coupled to the manuals.

In English-speaking countries, the bottom manual of a two-manual organ is traditionally called the 'Great' and the upper manual the 'Swell'. If there is a third manual it is the 'Choir', below the Great; and if there is a fourth it is the 'Solo', above the Swell. The pipes belonging to the Swell (and sometimes the Choir and Solo) are enclosed in a box. One side of the box is made like a Venetian blind and can be opened and closed by a separate pedal, normally above the pedal-board, producing the effect of a *crescendo* or *diminuendo*. Modern organs modelled after the organs of J. S. Bach's time tend to discard the terms Great, Swell etc. in favour of German equivalents such as *Hauptwerk, Oberwerk* and *Positiv.*

Organ pipes can be divided into two main categories: flue pipes, which – however large they may be – are basically whistles (like recorders), and reed pipes, in which the sound is produced by the wind causing a tongue of reed (actually made of metal) to vibrate.

Ranks of pipes are classified according to the length (and hence the pitch) of the lowest note. 𝄢 (the lowest note on the manuals and also on the pedal-board) is produced by a pipe eight feet (8′) long, so a rank of pipes with this as its bottom note would be called an 8′ stop. A pipe twice as long (16′) produces a note an octave lower,[1] and a rank of pipes with this as its bottom note is therefore a 16′ stop, sounding an octave lower than an 8′ stop. Similarly, a 4′ stop sounds an octave higher than the written notes, and a 2′ stop two octaves higher. 'Mutation' stops sound at other intervals than the octave or octaves, such as the 12th or 17th: their effect is to add brilliance when they are combined with 8′ stops. 'Mixture' stops have two or more pipes per note – sometimes as many as five: a mixture of 8′, octave and mutation pipes. They, too, add brilliance.

The name of each stop appears on its draw-stop (or stop-key) together with a figure indicating the pitch at which it sounds, e.g. 'Open Diapason 8' 'Bourdon 16', 'Principal 4'. Stops are often named after orchestral instruments which they purport to imitate: 'Flute', 'Oboe', 'Trumpet', for example. Organs vary enormously in the number and character of their stops, so composers rarely specify 'registration' (i.e. a particular choice of stops) exactly; mostly they leave it entirely to the player to decide.

Organ music is written on three staves: the upper two for the manuals and the bottom one for the pedals. The bar-lines are broken between the two lowest staves thus –

Vaughan Williams, *Rhosymedre*

Andantino

Soft Swell 8′ & 4′

etc.

Soft 16′ coupled to Sw.

[1] A flue pipe can be made to sound an octave lower by closing it at the end. Thus an 8′ rank of 'stopped' pipes would sound at 16′ pitch and would be classified as a 16′ stop.

21/3d Electric keyboards

Instruments whose sounds are dependent upon the use of electricity have
been in existence since the closing years of the 19th century, and have become
increasingly popular since the middle of the 20th. They can be divided into
two broad categories:

1) Those whose sounds, however tiny, are made by conventional means
(usually strings) and then amplified. These are 'electro-acoustic' instruments
– the electro-acoustic guitar used in pop groups is a familiar example.

2) Those whose sounds are generated by purely electronic means, such as
oscillators. Only these are strictly 'electronic' instruments.

One result of these developments has been the production of cheaper and
more portable substitutes for traditional keyboard instruments. Pianos using
both principles have been made, though few people would claim that they are
an adequate replacement for the genuine article. Much more successful is the
electronic organ. In many churches it has replaced the pipe organ and – since
it is a close imitation – is played in the same way and uses the same
terminology, nothing more needs to be said about that particular variety.
Rather different are the electronic organs mainly intended for entertainment
in the home and which cannot be used for the performance of conventional
organ music. They are usually two-manual instruments with shorter
keyboards, the upper one offset to the right of the lower one, and a shorter
pedal-board (a single octave from the bottom C). Percussion effects with
regularly repeating rhythms can be produced automatically, and there are
other devices such as simplified ways of playing chords.

The use of the old-fashioned keyboard to play electronic sounds has made
available a variety of what are really new instruments, ranging from little
light-weight toys to the full-scale synthesizer. Basically, this generates the
simplest constituents of single sounds which it then combines and modifies in
an infinite variety of ways, producing a vast spectrum of pitch, dynamics, tone
colours and rhythmic patterns.

CHAPTER 22

Instruments in combination

Instruments can be combined to form chamber-music groups, orchestras and bands.

22/1 Chamber-music groups

The essential difference between chamber music and music for an orchestra or band is that in chamber music there is only one player for each part: the instruments are not duplicated, so if a player is missing there is a hole in the music. Because chamber music is played by soloists it has a particularly intimate quality. Although often performed nowadays in concert halls, it is really music designed to be played in a room rather than in a large public auditorium. The word 'chamber' is actually derived from the Latin word for 'room': *camera*.

Naturally, only a few players are involved. Nevertheless, music for just one or two players (e.g. a piano sonata or a sonata for violin and piano) is not normally described as chamber music. Ordinarily at least three players are implied, while at the other extreme there are scarcely ever more than eight. A group of three players is a **trio**, four are a **quartet**, five a **quintet**, six a **sextet**, seven a **septet** and eight an **octet**. The words 'trio', 'quartet' etc. are used in two senses, referring both to the number of players and to the music itself. A 'string quartet', for example, can mean either a group of four musicians who play string instruments or a sonata for four string instruments.

Most chamber music is in fact written for strings. A **string trio** normally consists of a violin, a viola and a cello[1], while a **string quartet** (the most popular of all chamber-music groups) includes two violins, a viola and a cello (the opening of Debussy's String Quartet is printed on the next page as an example). Larger string groups may vary a little. A **string quintet**, for instance, may add either a second viola or a second cello to the string quartet.

When strings are combined with a piano or with some other instrument[2], the resulting combination takes its name from the additional instrument. Thus a **piano trio** is a group consisting of a piano, a violin and a cello – not

[1] In the baroque period, a 'trio sonata' usually implied two solo instruments, e.g. violins, plus continuo (usually a cello and harpsichord) – *four* players in all. See Part I, p.63.
[2] A few composers have also written for a combination which includes a solo voice, e.g. Vaughan Williams' *On Wenlock Edge* for tenor, string quartet and piano.

Debussy, String Quartet (1st mvt)

three pianos[1], and a **piano quartet** is a piano plus a violin, viola and cello. A **piano quintet** is normally a piano plus the usual string quartet, although one of the most famous of piano quintets, Schubert's 'Trout' Quintet, is written for piano, violin, viola, cello and double bass. Similarly, an **oboe quartet** or a **clarinet quartet** includes an oboe or a clarinet together with a violin, viola and cello, while in a **clarinet quintet** the wind instrument is combined with a string quartet[2].

Wind-only combinations are much more unusual. In fact only one is at all common: the **wind quintet**, normally consisting of a flute, an oboe, a clarinet, a bassoon and a horn. Combinations of wind groups and piano are also quite rare, though amongst them is one of Mozart's greatest works, his Quintet for piano, oboe, clarinet, horn and bassoon.

Composers write chamber music in open score (see p.108); individual players, however, usually have just their own part in front of them (as they do in an orchestra). When the piano is combined with other instruments, its part is written below theirs in the score; and it is from the score that the pianist plays. If strings and wind are combined, the wind parts are written above the strings. Bar-lines are ruled without a break through all the staves belonging to instruments of the same kind (wind or strings or piano) but not between instruments of different kinds.

22/2 Orchestras

The dividing-line between a chamber-music group and an orchestra can be fine but it is nevertheless real. Nowadays 'orchestra' is taken to mean a group of instruments which always includes strings (though usually other instruments as well), each of the string parts being played by *several* performers, not by soloists. A **string orchestra** is one which consists only of strings, divided into first and second violins, violas, cellos and double basses. Since there is more than one player to each part, the parts can be sub-divided. When this happens, the music is marked *divisi* (or just *div.*); when they come together again, it is marked *unis.* ('in unison').

The expression **chamber orchestra** is merely an unnecessarily confusing

---

[1] Just to complicate matters, a 'piano duet' is two pianists playing on one piano! A sonata for piano duet is therefore not the same as a sonata for two pianos.

[2] To demonstrate the variety of combinations in the output of one composer, Brahms wrote: three trios for violin, cello and piano; a trio for clarinet (or viola), cello and piano; a trio for violin, horn (or viola) and piano; three quartets for 2 violins, viola and cello; three quartets for violin, viola, cello and piano; two quintets for 2 violins, 2 violas and cello; a quintet for 2 violins, viola, cello and piano; a quintet for clarinet, 2 violins, viola and cello; and two sextets for 2 violins, 2 violas and 2 cellos.

way of referring to a small orchestra which includes other instruments as well as strings: the music it plays is not chamber music. By modern standards *all* early orchestras were small orchestras. In the early 17th century they were variable collections of instruments, but gradually they became more standardised. By J. S. Bach's time, strings together with a continuo instrument (see Part I, p.63) had emerged as the basis to which other instruments might be added; by the end of the 18th century the continuo had discarded and the orchestra had settled into what is essentially its modern form – even though it was still to grow a great deal larger. In this modern form, the 'full orchestra' or 'symphony orchestra' is customarily divided into four sections – strings, woodwind, brass and percussion.

The divisions are not entirely clear-cut. Horns, for example, form a group of their own, for although they clearly do not belong to the woodwind section, neither are they generally regarded as belonging to the brass section of the orchestra: the brass section includes only the 'heavy brass' instruments – trumpets, trombones and tubas. Somewhat similarly, the percussion section does not conventionally include the timpani. Furthermore, some instruments which are 19th- or 20th-century additions to the orchestra cannot be neatly slotted into any of the usual categories. The harp is a case in point: although it is unquestionably a string instrument, it is plainly different from the violins etc. and does not form part of the string section of the orchestra.

Nevertheless, although blurred at the edges, the division of orchestral instruments into sections is still broadly applicable, as can be seen from a comparison of the orchestras required for two works written over a century apart: Beethoven's Symphony No.3 in E♭ ('Eroica'), composed in 1803–4, and Bartók's *Concerto for Orchestra*[1] (1944). On the opposite page the instruments are listed exactly as they appear in the **full score**[2] (a score which shows all the music for all the performers).

The precise number of strings required is scarcely ever specified by composers, though more and more have had to be used as other, and more powerful, instruments have been added to the orchestra. Typical figures for an orchestra today would be in the region of 14 first violins, 14 second violins, 12 violas, 10 cellos and 8 double basses. Other instruments have only one player each: '2 flutes', for example, indicates one flautist playing the first flute part and another the second flute part.

---

[1] Bartók called this a concerto and not a symphony because, although there is no single soloist, all the instruments at various times have a solo role.

[2] If a full score is reduced in size (but otherwise unaltered) it is variously called a 'miniature score', a 'pocket score' or a 'study score'. A 'piano score' is one in which the orchestral parts (and vocal parts if there are any) are shown in as much detail as possible on two staves, so that the music can be played on a piano. A 'set of parts' means the separate copies required by the individual players, giving only the music for their particular instruments.

Beethoven		**Bartók**
Symphony No.3 ('Eroica')		*Concerto for Orchestra*

Beethoven		Bartók
2 Flutes 2 Oboes 2 Clarinets in B♭ 2 Bassoons	WOODWIND	3 Flutes (3rd doubling Piccolo) 3 Oboes (3rd doubling Cor Anglais) 3 Clarinets in B♭ and A (3rd doubling Bass Clarinet) 3 Bassoons (3rd doubling Double Bassoon)
3 Horns in E♭		4 Horns in F
2 Trumpets in E♭ BRASS		3 Trumpets in C (4th Trumpet ad lib.) 2 Tenor Trombones Bass Trombone Tuba
2 Timpani		Timpani
	PERCUSSION	Side Drum Bass Drum Tam-tam Cymbals Triangle
		2 Harps
Violins I Violins II Violas Cellos Double Basses	STRINGS	Violins I Violins II Violas Cellos Double Basses

This tabulation also shows the standard order in which instruments are arranged in the score. The first page of the 'Eroica' Symphony is printed in full on p.234.

In its day, the orchestra for Beethoven's 'Eroica' was large: up till then only two horns were standard and his use of a third was exceptional. Nevertheless, Beethoven was to expand the symphony orchestra still further with the addition of a piccolo and three trombones[1] in the 5th Symphony and a fourth horn in the 9th, together with a triangle, cymbals and a bass drum (not to mention four solo singers and a chorus). Bartók's orchestra, on the other hand was by no means remarkable in the mid-20th century: composers such as Mahler and Richard Strauss had already called for far more resources around the beginning of the century.

[1] Trombones had been used earlier in opera (e.g. Mozart's *The Magic Flute*) and in church music (e.g. Mozart's Requiem Mass).

Beethoven, Symphony No. 3 (1st mvt)

Some details in the Bartók list may need explanation. 'Doubling' indicates that a performer has to play either of two instruments as required: the third flautist, for example, has to change to the piccolo when necessary. (The word is also used in a different sense: if one says, for instance, that the first violins are 'doubled' by the clarinets, this means that they both play the same music.) '4th Trumpet ad lib.' means that the fourth trumpet is not essential. The number of timpani is not specified but, since the music clearly requires pedal timps, two would be sufficient in spite of frequent changes of notes. A separate player is not needed for each of the percussion instruments; in fact in this work one player apart from the timpanist could manage them all.

In spite of their variations of detail, the two lists of instruments are entirely typical of the basic divisions of the orchestra and of the order in which the instruments are arranged in the score. Only a few additional points need to be made:

1) Until about the end of the 18th century the double basses usually played the same music as the cellos (though sounding an octave lower); hence they shared the same stave. Beethoven began to give them more independence and, when this happened, they needed a stave of their own; subsequently separate staves became the norm.

2) When a single line of music is to be played in unison by two or more instruments of the same kind (e.g. flutes), the stave is marked 'a 2' or 'a 3' etc.

3) In a full score, continuous bar-lines are drawn through instruments belonging to the same section (woodwind, brass etc.). The horns are barred together but separately from other instruments. Timpani have bar-lines to themselves; other percussion instruments may be barred together or independently. Harps and keyboard instruments (if any) always have their own bar-lines.

4) If there is a solo instrument (e.g. the piano in a piano concerto), its part is always placed immediately above the strings.

5) Voices (soloists and/or chorus) are nowadays also placed above the strings, although until the early 20th century they used to appear between the violas and the cellos.

6) In some 20th-century scores, transposing instruments are notated 'in C', i.e. at their concert pitch, although the separate parts for the individual players would normally be written with the necessary transpositions.

22/3 Bands

'Band' is a rather vague word which in the past has been used to refer to almost any sizeable collection of instrumentalists, even to what we would now call an orchestra. In modern usage the word generally implies a large group of wind and percussion players, such as **brass band** or a **military band**. Neither of these includes strings (for the very good reason that they normally play out of doors, where strings would be ineffective), but they are not the same. The essential difference is that brass bands do not include woodwind instruments but military bands do. Both include many instruments not normally found in the symphony orchestra (though usually related to those that are); both also vary somewhat from one country to another in the particular mixture of instruments.

The **symphonic wind band** (or **concert band**) is similar to a military band in including both woodwind and brass instruments, but as its name suggests it is free from associations with the parade-ground. Since about the middle of the 20th century, many leading composers (e.g. Prokofiev, Schoenberg and Copland) have been drawn to write for it in a wide variety of styles.

Pre-war jazz bands, dance bands, and the popular entertainment groups which later replaced them are much more variable, generally including some instruments outside the usual wind and percussion categories, such as the double bass, guitar and piano (or, more recently, electronic keyboard instruments). The West Indian 'steel bands' are essentially percussion bands, but their instruments (made with great skill out of the simplest resources, notably oil drums) are pitched and can produce remarkably elaborate textures.

CHAPTER 23

Before the tonal period

The account of chords and other harmonic considerations given in Chapters 8–9 (Part I) & 15–17 was a summary of the raw materials of the system of harmony which underlies most of the music we know. This system emerged very gradually, but in all essentials it was fully formed by the beginning of the 17th century. Its possibilities were so rich that for the next three hundred years composers were occupied in exploring it, developing it both as a source of expression and as a means of constructing large-scale musical forms.

Yet well before the end of the 19th century the work of some composers had begun to take them into new paths. There followed in the 20th century a period of rapid developments in various directions. A comprehensive account of these would be out of place here since this is not a history book; but an introduction to some of the most influential of them is needed because they led to quite new methods of composition, and to some innovations in notation.

One of the most striking features of modern music is how often one finds connections or parallels with music from *before* the tonal period, and indeed with other music which lies outside the familiar harmonic system, such as folksong and non-Western music. We can begin to bring these generalisations into sharper focus by first considering what is meant by **modes**.

Traditional modes

A major key and a minor key with the same key-note (e.g. C major and C minor) are said to be different 'modes' of the same key (see Part I, p.26). This is a rather special usage, however, for 'mode' also has wider and somewhat different connotations – as phrases such as 'modal music' and 'the modal system' suggest. The roots of Western music lie in the chants sung in the services of the early Church. These were the earliest and simplest examples of what became known as **plainsong** or 'plainchant' or (in the form standardised by the Roman Catholic Church) as 'Gregorian chant'. Medieval theorists divided plainsong into a number of categories or modes.[1] Because the modes originally applied to church music, they are sometimes called 'church modes' or 'ecclesiastical modes', although they are equally relevant to some other kinds

[1]The medieval scholars who wrote about modes were much influenced by the theories of ancient Greek writers on music – but by their theories, not by the actual music, which was unknown to them. Thus the names given to modes were taken from Greek music.

of music, particularly folksong. It is important to realise that modal theory was initially concerned with *melodies*, indeed *unaccompanied* melodies: the plainsong melodies to which it referred were in existence many centuries before the most rudimentary beginnings of harmony. The folksongs which have survived until our own times are not nearly as old, but they too were originally conceived as pure melodies, without harmony, even though professional musicians have frequently added accompaniments to them.

As an example of a modal melody, here is the start of a chant sung at Mass on Easter Sunday to Latin words beginning *Victimae paschali laudes*. As in all plainsong, the rhythm is not strict, but a suitable speed would be about ♪ =152. (Signs above the stave can for the moment be disregarded.)

At first glance this may look as though it is in C major; but as soon as it is sung or played, one realises that it does not *sound* like C major. Far from giving the impression of a 'home' note or tonic, the note C is not even particularly important. Yet neither is the melody in A minor or D minor. The fact is that it is not in a key at all, but in a mode: the particular mode called the **Dorian** mode. 'Dorian mode' was the term by which medieval theorists described all melodies using the notes of a white-note scale starting on D –

although, as will be seen, that is not in itself a complete explanation.

In the same way, the theorists gave names to modes using the notes of white-note scales starting on other notes: the **Phrygian**, starting on E –

the **Lydian**, starting on F; and the **Mixolydian**, starting on G. These modes were the only ones used in Gregorian chant, although, later, two other modes were recognised: the **Ionian**, starting on C, and the **Aeolian**, starting on A[1].

---

[1]For the sake of completeness, theorists were also tempted to invent a mode with a scale starting on B: the 'Locrian' mode. This was abandoned, however, since there was never any actual music in this mode!

It has to be said, however, that these two have less strongly defined characteristics than the other modes, and they seem to us, now, less clearly distinguishable from later major and minor keys (Ionian/C major; Aeolian/A minor).

Each mode was said to exist in two forms, **authentic** and **plagal**. The plagal form of the mode always lies a perfect 4th below (= a perfect 5th above) the authentic mode. The authentic form of the Dorian mode, for example, is from D to D, but its plagal form is from A to A –

Plagal modes were distinguished by the prefix 'Hypo-' (Greek for 'under'): Hypodorian, Hypophrygian etc. Plainsong books used in churches, however, identify modes not by names but by numbers. The authentic modes have odd numbers, and the plagal modes have even numbers: the Dorian mode is 'Mode 1', the Hypodorian mode is 'Mode 2', and so on.

The first note of each modal scale in its authentic form is called its 'final' (not 'tonic'). The final was unchanged in the plagal form. D is the final of both the Dorian and the Hypodorian modes, therefore, and the Hypodorian mode (final of D) is not the same as the Aeolian mode (final on A). But theorists went on to single out a note of secondary importance in each mode, a note variously

AUTHENTIC MODES	PLAGAL MODES	MODE NUMBER	RANGE	FINAL	TENOR or DOMINANT
Dorian		1	D–D	D	A
	Hypodorian	2	A–A	D	F
Phrygian		3	E–E	E	C
	Hypophrygian	4	B–B	E	A
Lydian		5	F–F	F	C
	Hypolydian	6	C–C	F	A
Mixolydian		7	G–G	G	D
	Hypomixolydian	8	D–D	G	C
Aeolian		9	A–A	A	E
	Hypoaeolian	10	E–E	A	C
Ionian		11	C–C	C	G
	Hypoionian	12	G–G	C	E

referred to as the 'tenor' (from the Latin word for 'to hold') or 'reciting note' –
because of its importance in chanting psalms – or as the 'dominant'. This note
was *not* the same in both the authentic and plagal forms of the mode; nor was it
always at the same interval from the final, as can be seen from the table on the
previous page.

Unfortunately, the traditional theory outlined in the table does not always
fit the facts of the music itself. The *Victimae paschali* melody quoted on p.238,
for example, later includes this phrase –

thus, the total range of the whole piece is an octave and a 4th, so it is apparently
both authentic *and* plagal! And the beautiful hymn, *Jesu dulcis memoria*, which
is also in the Dorian mode, ends on the dominant, not the final –

Clearly there must be other factors apart from the range of a melody and its
final which give it its particular modal character.

The solution to the puzzle is a matter of some subtlety, yet of considerable
importance. What all the melodies of a particular mode have in common is
certain melodic shapes or outlines. The Dorian mode, for example, is
characterised by patterns such as these –

Two or more of these cells may be combined, and the notes within them may
be used in any order. Gaps between notes are often filled out by passing-notes,
so that the cell-notes themselves become as it were the skeleton of the melody.
Yet the basic patterns are persistent and easily recognisable. In the examples
from *Victimae paschali* and *Jesu dulcis memoria* quoted above, these basic
patterns are marked by asterisks.

The same outlines appear if we turn to a different source: folksong, e.g. the Dorian-mode melody of an English folksong, 'The Royal Oak' –

It is contours such as these which give Dorian-mode melodies their special flavour, which is quite unlike the flavour of, say, the Phrygian or Mixolydian modes, which have distinctive melodic shapes of their own.[1]

Plainsong and folksong modes, then, are not quite the same as scales. A mode is a complex of melodic patterns. The notes used in these patterns can be arranged in order to form a one-octave modal scale (e.g. those already quoted), but this is merely a device of theorists: modal melodies themselves never include such scales. Sometimes, indeed, they do not even use all the notes contained in the theoretical modal scale. The following folksong[2], for example, is clearly in the Dorian mode, but it uses only the notes D, F, G, A and C: E and B do not occur –

[1] Similar (though not always the same) melodic shapes are found in the folksongs of other Western countries. Indeed, melodic construction of this kind is almost universal: something very like it is found in the traditional music of countries all over the world, e.g. in the *rāgs* of Indian music.

[2] 'Edward', from *80 English Folk Songs*, collected by Cecil Sharp and Maud Karpeles (Faber & Faber, 1968).

If the notes of this melody are arranged in order, they produce a **gapped**

scale –  – the 'gaps' being at

the points marked **x**. This particular melody is said to be **pentatonic**, meaning that it uses only five different notes. Pentatonic melodies are common in folksong: more familiar examples (though not in the Dorian mode) are 'Auld Lang Syne' and 'Old Macdonald had a farm'. Even more common are melodies which are nearly pentatonic because they are built mainly from five notes, the other two being rare and given little importance.

Plainsong melodies and secular folksongs existed long before a method of writing them down had been invented. They would have been sung at any pitch which was convenient. Early notation could show only the relationship

of notes to each other, so , for example, represented the interval of

a perfect 5th, but not necessarily the particular pitches which these notes would produce on a modern piano. As music became more elaborate, however, and fixed-pitch instruments like organs were invented, notation began to imply precise pitches (even though it was not until the 20th century that a more or less universal agreement on a standard pitch was achieved). Composers who based their music on the old plainsong melodies did not always want to use them at the exact pitch which the written notes had come to mean, and so they transposed them when necessary. Sixteenth-century composers (e.g. Palestrina) generally used only one transposition: up a perfect 4th with a Bb added at the beginning as a 'key' signature. Later composers have transposed them to any convenient pitch. For example, the Dorian-mode plainsong melody *Dies irae* (sung at funerals) which begins

appears thus in the 'Witches' Sabbath' of the *Symphonie Fantastique* by Berlioz (played in unison by two tubas and four bassoons!) –

CHAPTER 24

Some modern developments

24/1 The undermining of tonal harmony

When Berlioz used the *Dies irae* theme he was making a special dramatic effect by quoting an ancient melody which his listeners would have known and would have associated with death. Modal melodies were not part of the standard musical language of his day. Indeed, they are largely irreconcilable with the harmonic system of the entire tonal period. The modal system (which, it must be stressed again, was essentially to do with *melody*) had been more and more compromised as *harmony* evolved throughout the centuries. When modal melodies were harmonised, accidentals began to be applied to notes because this suited the harmony better, in spite of the fact that accidentals often destroyed the characteristic modal contours of the music. Perhaps even more importantly, harmony began to produce melodic shapes of its own: the notes of chords arranged as melodies (see 18/2). By the early 17th century, modal melodies had almost completely given way to melodies which not only fitted more easily into progressions of chords but often grew out of them.

Yet the battle was to break out again. In the second half of the 19th century, composers in Russia began to react against the domination of their music by that of other countries. In seeking a way of composing which was distinctively Russian, they turned to their native folk music. Composers such as Borodin, Balakirev and Mussorgsky not only harmonised folksongs, they also incorporated them into original compositions and in a broader way adopted their characteristic idioms as a basis for a new musical style. The influence of folk music on professionally composed music inevitably affected not only melody but harmony too. Rather than distort the characteristic shapes of modal melodies, composers preferred to use familiar chords in new ways, devising new cadences and harmonic progressions.

Similar developments took place in other countries and became part of a much wider exploration for new ways of writing music. Even composers who were not directly moved by folksong and plainsong were quick to recognise in them the subtleties of melodies not geared to chords, and the possibilities they suggested of harmonies not governed by old notions of cadences and other progressions. The passage quoted on p.124 from Debussy's piano prelude, *La Cathédrale engloutie*, for example, uses traditional chords but in a quite new way – simply a succession of second-inversion chords moving completely parallel with the melody. Plainsong melodies had been 'harmonised' by the addition of parallel melodic lines as early as the 9th century (a technique known as **organum**), but such passages had never before been written in the tonal period.

Not only were established ideas of chordal progressions jettisoned. Also abandoned was an essential principle of harmony of the tonal period: that discords (e.g. the 7th in a dominant 7th chord) must be resolved. This can be seen in a later extract from the same prelude –

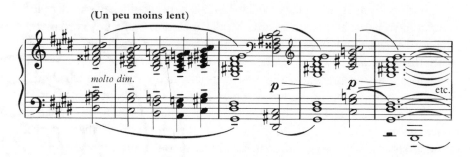

From here it was but a short step to the invention of chords no longer derived from triads made up of thirds (see 8/1–2 in Part I). Skryabin and others constructed chords out of fourths, as in this passage from Bartók's *Sonata for two pianos and percussion* –

Indeed, no combination of notes was thought to be intrinsically impossible although, as we shall see shortly, new scales and other developments were to lead to the replacement of the old system of harmony by new methods of organisation.

First, however, another departure from traditional practices must be mentioned: **polytonality** – the use of more than one key *simultaneously*. **Bitonality** (the use of two keys at once) is simply one kind of polytonality, though the most common. Bartók again provides an illustration, the opening of his first Bagatelle for piano –

© Copyright Editio Musica Budapest

Bitonality is clearly signalled here by the different key-signatures, but these are not essential: the same effect can be achieved with a common key-signature (or none) by the addition of the necessary accidentals before the individual notes.

24/2 Modern scales and modes

New departures such as those we have seen above undermined the long-standing domination of the major and minor scales as the basis of musical composition. What was to demolish this domination completely was the use of quite different principles of selecting and organising the raw materials of music, the pitches of the notes from which it is made. An example is the **whole-tone scale**, i.e. one consisting entirely of intervals of a tone –

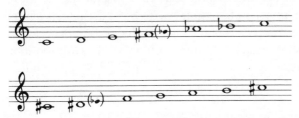

(In the notation of the whole-tone scale and other scales about to be discussed, any note can be written as an enharmonic equivalent, e.g. either F♯ or G♭. This is simply a matter of convenience and has no other significance.)

The whole-tone scale had occasionally been combined with conventional harmonic progressions based on diatonic scales in the 19th century (particularly in Russia), and – though very rarely – even earlier. It was not until the 20th century, however, that music was written which used *only* the notes of the whole-tone scale. Debussy's piano prelude, *Voiles* (Veils), is a celebrated example. This quotation from it starts in bar 10 –

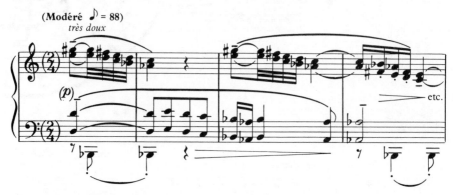

The somewhat mysterious impression which this music creates arises out of the fact that the listener is deprived of the usual bearings. Since the notes of the whole-tone scale are the same distance apart, they all seem to be of equal importance. None automatically stands out as a tonic or dominant.

Two examples of the whole-tone scale are given above: one starting on C, one on C♯. Starting a whole-tone scale on D or any other note merely produces the same notes as one or another of these two. In the music of Olivier Messiaen the whole-tone scale is but one of a number of what he called **modes of limited transposition**. He was careful to point out that these 'modes' have nothing to do with the modes of plainsong and folksong. But neither are they like major or minor scales, or even the theoretical modal scales. The most important difference is that in all of them – not just in the whole-tone scale – no note is more important than the others. In particular, the first note of each is in no sense a 'tonic' or 'final'.

According to Messiaen, the whole-tone scale (the first of his modes of limited transposition) is 'transposable twice': a rather misleading way of saying that there are only two versions of it which produce different notes, i.e. the original position (which he called 'first transposition') and its transposition either up or down a semitone (the 'second transposition'). His second mode of limited transposition is –

(first transposition)

This has three transpositions, i.e. transposing the original to start on C♯ or D results in different groups of notes –

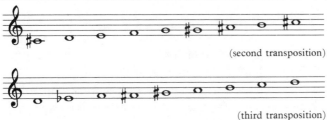

(second transposition)

(third transposition)

but any other transposition would merely produce the notes already contained in one of the first three.

Closer inspection of this particular mode shows that it is made up of four units, each consisting of a semitone followed by a tone, with the last note of each unit becoming the first of the next –

In Messiaen's theory there are seven modes of limited transposition. They vary in the number of notes they contain, but all have a similar symmetrical arrangement. Mode 3, for example, which has four transpositions, is

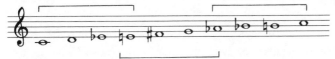

Messiaen explained his technique of composition in a book which was translated into English as *The technique of my musical language*[1]. He quotes the following passage from *Les sons impalpables du rêve* (the fifth of his piano preludes) as an example of his use of modes of limited transposition. Here it is the second mode in the first transposition which is employed. This has already been set out opposite, but it has to be remembered that in practice notes are sometimes 'spelt' differently by the substitution of enharmonic equivalents.

To prevent misunderstandings, Messiaen has included many accidentals which are not strictly required.

[1] *Technique de mon langage musical* (Alphonse Leduc, Paris 1944; English translation, 1957)

24/3 The twelve-note method

Other composers had followed a different route in moving away from the
tonal period's principles of chords, harmonic progressions and keys. Their
way had been prepared during the later part of the 19th century, particularly
in Germany, when increasing use was made of chromatic notes and chords
(see Chapter 17). In itself the use of chromaticism was nothing new:
J. S. Bach and many others before and after him had exploited its expressive
possibilities. But its more extensive use in the 19th century by composers such
as Wagner reached the point where the sense of a fixed tonic began to
disappear. Once this anchorage was weakened, the feeling of music being in a
key became less and less secure, as these bars from Wagner's *Die Walküre*
illustrate –

In this passage a number of features, notably the way in which the music
cadences on to common chords of E major and C major, still give us the
impression that the music has tonality (a feeling of being in a key), albeit
changing quickly. When, however, the process was pushed even further in the
early years of the 20th century, and such cadences and common chords were
avoided, the resulting music was **atonal**, i.e. no note stood out as a tonic and
there was therefore no sense of key.

Nevertheless, it was quickly realised that merely abandoning the practice of
tonal harmony was not in itself a way forward. Some other means of
organising music had to be found, one which accepted and ensured the
equality of all twelve notes of the chromatic scale and yet produced a new kind
of cohesion to replace tonality. The most far-reaching and fully worked-out
solution to the problem was devised by Schoenberg in what he described as a
'Method of composing with twelve notes which are related only with one
another': a system also known as 'dodecaphony' or, more loosely, as 'serial
technique'.

A piece of music which uses this method has as its basis a 'series' (or 'note
row') comprising all twelve notes of the chromatic scale, arranged in any order
the composer wishes. Schoenberg, for example, used this series in his
Variations for Orchestra, Op.31 –

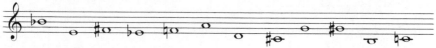

From the original series three others can be derived. The first is its mirror-image: ascending intervals become descending intervals and vice versa. Thus an ascending major 3rd, for example, becomes a descending major 3rd. This mirrored form is called the 'inversion'[1] of the original series. In the notation it is immaterial how the notes are spelt since they do not have the function in scales and chords which they have in tonal music. (For the same reason, double sharps and flats are not used at all.) This has to be kept in mind when comparing the original series above with its inversion –

The other two series are obtained by reversing the notes (i.e. playing them backwards) of the original series and of its inversions. These back-to-front arrangements are called 'retrogrades' of the original and of its inversion.

All four series (original, inversion, retrograde original, retrograde inversion) can be transposed to start on any of the twelve degrees of the chromatic scale. Thus altogether there are 48 versions of the original pattern of notes available (which is not to say that all 48 have to be used!). Moreover, any note may be played at any octave, i.e. one or more octaves higher or lower. But in none of its forms is a series to be thought of as a theme or a melody: rather it provides a succession of notes from which not only melodies but also chords can be made. Chords are the result of playing adjacent notes of a series simultaneously. The opening (bars 34–38) of the theme of Schoenberg's *Variations*[2] illustrates the application of his series –

Molto moderato (♩ = 88)

[1]This is not to be confused with the sense in which the word 'inversion' is applied to harmonic intervals and triads (see 7/4 and 8/1 in Part I). See also p.189.

[2]In Schoenberg's score, the second and third notes in the melody (E, F♯) appear as F♭ and G♭: they have been rewritten here to facilitate comparison with the note-row opposite. Also, accidentals which are unnecessary (according, at least to the conventions of tonal harmony) have been omitted, although Schoenberg and his followers made it a practice to put an accidental before *every* note: thus, for example, there is a ♮ before the first note (G in the bass clef) in the original.

Here the melody (in the treble clef) uses the series in its original form, while the notes of the chords (in the bass clef) are those of the inversion transposed to start on G –

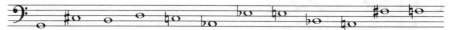

The notes of a single series may be distributed throughout the texture, some appearing in the melody, some in the bass or other parts. Thus a melodic line is not itself bound to include all twelve notes of a series. But wherever they are used, all the notes in a series must be heard before it is repeated or one of its alternative versions begun. This preserves the integrity of the series as a whole, which Schoenberg saw as a cohesive force akin to that of tonality in earlier music.

24/4 Rhythm

The 20th-century's departures from tonality were matched by departures from earlier ideas of rhythm. With scarcely any exceptions, music of the tonal period was characterised by regularly recurring beats and accents, indicated by the time signature and bar-lines. This underlying pattern is sometimes referred to as the metre of the music. Devices such as syncopation (see 6/3 in Part I) made their effect precisely because they were temporary contradictions of the basic metre: without it they would have been pointless. Not all music is based on a regular metre, however. Plainsong is not; nor, frequently, is folk music.

Folksong, indeed, was a powerful influence inspiring many late 19th- and early 20th-century composers to more flexible uses of rhythm in their own music. A little later, some composers took up ideas of rhythmic organisation from the medieval period, while others looked to non-Western music. Messiaen, for example, owed much to Hindu theories in formulating his own ideas about rhythm. These were not only demonstrated in his compositions but also explained in his *The technique of my musical language*. Although they are too involved and extensive to be discussed fully here, it is perhaps not too sweeping to say that they provided a systematic basis for the use of ametrical (non-metrical) rhythm. One detail of his theories provided a striking parallel to his modes of limited transposition: the idea of **non-retrogradable rhythms**. These are rhythmic patterns whose time values remain the same if they are reversed. Each bar of the following passage (from the *Quartet for the end of time*) provides a different example –

Here, as in much of Messiaen's music, the use of a time signature has been abandoned altogether.

Later developments in 20th-century music were to take the serial methods, which Schoenberg had applied to note-pitches, and adapt them to time values and, indeed, to dynamic levels as well. But there were also reactions to this increasing systemisation, reactions which gave a quite new freedom to performers. Both paths led to the necessity for new devices of notation.

24/5 Notation

Not all the new methods of notation have become standard practice, and composers frequently provide explanations of how their written signs are to be interpreted. Here, however, are some 20th-century symbols which may often be encountered:

Notes of imprecise pitch, e.g. in spoken rhythms.

Notes to be performed simultaneously on the keyboard.

'Cluster' chords played on the white notes of the keyboard: *all* the white notes between the outer limits shown are to be played.

Cluster chords to be similarly played on the black notes.

Chromatic cluster chords, i.e. including both black and white notes.

A sign used by Schoenberg and some other twelve-note composers to indicate the principal melodic line.

A sign similarly used to show a subsidiary melody: the end of the passage is marked ⌐‾‾‾⌐ in each case.

An *accelerando* during a group of notes in free rhythm.

A *rallentando* during a group of notes in free rhythm.

Repeat the notes in the frame freely for as long as the wavy line indicates. (Sometimes a thick straight line is used instead.)

APPENDIX C

Names of orchestral instruments in English, Italian, German and French

English	Italian	German	French
flute	flauto, or flauto grande	Flöte, or grosse Flöte	flûte, or grande flûte
piccolo	flauto piccolo, or ottavino	kleine Flöte	petite flûte
alto flute, or bass flute, or flute in G	flauto contralto	Altflöte	flûte en sol
oboe	oboe	Oboe or Hoboe	hautbois
cor anglais, or English horn	corno inglese	Englischhorn	cor anglais
oboe d'amore	oboe d'amore	Liebesoboe	hautbois d'amour
clarinet	clarinetto	Klarinette	clarinette
bass clarinet	clarinetto basso, or clarone	Bassklarinette	clarinette basse
bassoon	fagotto	Fagott	basson
double bassoon, or contrabassoon	contrafagotto	Kontrafagott	contrebasson
horn, or French horn	corno	Horn (pl. Hörner)	cor
natural horn	corno naturale	Waldhorn	cor simple
valve horn	corno ventile, or corno cromatico	Ventilhorn	cor à pistons, or cor chromatique
trumpet	tromba (pl. trombe)	Trompete	trompette
cornet	cornetta	Kornett	cornet à pistons
trombone	trombone (pl. tromboni)	Posaune	trombone
tuba	tuba	Tuba	tuba
kettle drums	timpani	Pauken	timbales
side drum, or snare drum	tamburo piccolo, or tamburo militare	kleine Trommel	caisse claire, or tambour militaire
bass drum	cassa, or gran cassa	grosse Trommel	grosse caisse

English	Italian	German	French
cymbals	piatti, or cinelli	Becken	cymbales
gong	gong	Gong	gong
tam-tam	tam-tam	Tam-tam	tam-tam
triangle	triangolo	Triangel	triangle
tambourine	tamburino, or tamburo basco	Tamburin, or Schellentrommel	tambour de Basque
bells	campane	Glocken	cloches
glockenspiel	campanelli	Glockenspiel	jeu de timbres, or carillon
xylophone	xilofono, or silofono	Xylophon	xylophone
vibraphone	vibrafono	Vibraphone	vibraphone
celesta	celesta	Celesta	célesta
harp	arpa	Harfe	harpe
violin	violino	Violine, or Geige	violon
viola	viola	Bratsche	alto
cello	violoncello	Violoncello	violoncelle
double bass, or bass	contrabasso, or basso	Kontrabass	contrebasse

APPENDIX D

Roman chord-indications

1 Basic roman

The basic system (adopted throughout this book) of using roman numerals to describe triads and chords is outlined in Part I, pp.57 and 61. This system was originally devised to fit relatively simple, diatonic triads and chords, and was intended to do little more than to show the degrees of the scale on which their roots were based. It can be summarised as follows:

a)   Unless otherwise indicated, all notes are understood to belong to the major scale or (in a minor key) to the *harmonic* minor scale.

b)   Roman numerals in capital letters from I to VII denote the degree of the scale on which a triad (or the chord derived from it) is based.

c)   If a 7th is added to the basic triad, (as in the dominant 7th chord), a 7 is added to the right of the roman numeral – e.g. V^7. 9th, 11th and 13th chords may be similarly indicated (e.g. V^9, V^{11}, V^{13}).

d)   A first inversion chord is shown by 'b' after the roman numeral, a second inversion by 'c', a third inversion (as in a 7th chord) by 'd', and so on in the case of 9th, 11th and 13th chords.

e)   A ♭ before the roman numeral indicates that the root has been lowered a chromatic semitone (as in the major chord on the flattened supertonic). A♯ indicates that it has been raised a chromatic semitone. Note that ♭ and ♯ signs are used whatever the key signature: for example: ♭II indicates a chord on the flattened supertonic – even in, say, E major, where the actual root would be F♮.

An additional feature which may sometimes be found is an indication that a minor chord has been chromatically altered to become major (e.g. the major chord on the supertonic), but not all writers use the same symbol for this. Most add a ♯ after the roman numeral (e.g. II♯). Others write the numeral in italics (e.g. *II*), though this is perhaps best avoided since it can easily be confused, even when printed.

Fundamentally, however, the basic system makes no attempt to indicate whether triads and chords are major or minor etc. Moreover, it is not adequate to describe more complex chords, particularly chromatic chords. Other symbols have therefore been introduced to enable chords to be described with greater precision. Essentially there have been two different approaches to the problem. One – which for convenience will be called 'extended roman' – develops the basic system to enable it to show in detail whether chords are major, minor, augmented or diminished. The other – which may be called 'figured roman' – is a combination of the basic system with figured bass notation (as outlined in Part I, 8/4).

The notes below summarise the principal features of these two systems. It should be noted that they attach quite different meanings to certain symbols (e.g. +, – and °): hence it is essential not to attempt to combine extended roman and figured roman.

2 Extended roman

This differs from the basic system in the following respects:

a) Roman numerals in capital letters are reserved for chords with a *major* 3rd.

b) Roman numerals in lower-case letters (e.g. i, ii, vi) are used for chords with a *minor* 3rd.

c) Except where shown otherwise, the 5th from the root is perfect. A + sign after the roman numeral indicates an augmented 5th, and a ° sign in the same position (e.g. vii°) indicates a chord with a diminished 5th. In some books, a stroke (e.g. V') is used instead of a +.

d) When arabic figures (e.g. 7, 9 etc.) are added to indicate intervals from the root (e.g. V⁷), they are assumed to refer to notes of the appropriate scale (either major or harmonic minor) unless an accidental is added. To lower or raise the note by a chromatic semitone, a ♭ or a ♯ (irrespective of the key signature) is inserted before the arabic figure.

The following examples illustrate these usages –

Diatonic chords

Chords containing notes outside the major and harmonic minor scales

3 Figured roman

a) Roman numerals are used only in capitals. (Note that there are no special symbols to distinguish major, minor, augmented and diminished chords.)

b) To indicate a root which has been chromatically altered, a – is placed before the roman numeral if the root has been lowered a semitone, and a + if it has been raised a semitone. When the root of a minor chord is raised, the 3rd above it is assumed to be raised also; and when the root of a minor chord is lowered, the 5th above it is assumed to be lowered also.

c) A figure placed after the roman numeral indicates an interval *from the bass note* (i.e. as in a figured bass). An accidental placed either after or before this figure shows that the note it represents is to be chromatically altered (again as in a figured bass). Note that the accidental used is the one required by the actual note: figured roman differs from extended roman in this respect.

d) A ° is sometimes placed after the roman numeral to indicate that the latter refers to a theoretical root which is not in fact present in the chord. Thus a diminished seventh chord on the leading note of a major key, for example, could be shown as V$^{o}_{9}$b as well as VII^{7b}.

These are examples of the use of figured roman chord-indications –

APPENDIX E

Pitch Specifications

For some purposes – such as instrument manufacture and tuning – it is convenient to refer to the pitch of individual notes by a system of letter names. Two systems may be encountered: the first is the standard method, though it can be notated in two different ways (1a and 1b); the second is the traditional method used by English organ builders.

1a	C″	D″	E″ to	B″	C′	B′	C	B	c	b
1b	C_2	D_2	E_2 to	B_2	C_1	B_1	C_0	B_0	c^0	b^0
2	CCCC	DDDD	EEEE to	BBBB	CCC	BBB	CC	BB	C	B

1a	c′	b′	c″	b″	c‴	b‴	c⁗	b⁗	c′′′′′
1b	c^1	b^1	c^2	b^2	c^3	b^3	c^4	b^4	c^5
2	c	b	c′	b′	c″	b″	c‴	b‴	c⁗

APPENDIX F

Clefs

All of the following clefs (with middle C shown in brackets) were used in the 16th century. Some survived for many years, but only those marked * are still in use –

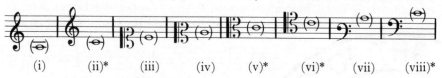

    (i)   (ii)*   (iii)   (iv)   (v)*   (vi)*   (vii)   (viii)*

It prevents confusion if they are referred to by the line of the stave on which they are placed: thus (i) = G1, (ii) = G2, (iii) = C1, (iv) = C2, (v) = C3, (vi) = C4, (vii) = F3, (viii) = F4. However, they have traditional names which are still in common use:

   (i) French violin clef or French treble clef (used extensively by French composers of the 17th and 18th centuries and by composers such as J. S. Bach for recorders and a small violin known as the 'piccolo' violin)
  (ii) treble clef
 (iii) soprano clef (often used by J. S. Bach for the right hand in his keyboard music, and up to the end of the 19th century for the soprano part in choral music)
  (iv) mezzo-soprano clef
   (v) alto clef
  (vi) tenor clef
 (vii) baritone clef
(viii) bass clef

A different way of drawing C clefs may be met, particularly in older editions –

 etc.

This is not standard, and its use is not recommended.

INDEX

mordent 114
motif 187–9
mute
— (on strings) 200
— (in wind instruments) 217

Neapolitan sixth chord 153–4
ninth chords 137–9
node 201–2
non-harmony notes (defined) 110
nota cambiata 115
notation (modern developments in)
251–2

oboe 209–10, 233–4
octet 229
open (string) 198
orchestra 231–5
orchestral chimes (see tubular bells)
organ
—, electronic 228
—, pipe 226–7
organum 244
overlap (of phrases) 186
overtones 201, 213

parallel motion 129–32, 136, 243–4
part-writing 129–32
partials 213
passing notes 110–3, 118, 123, 128,
134, 136–7, 149, 152
pedal-board 226–8
pedal mechanism
— (bass drum) 221
— (cymbal) 222
— (harp) 204
— (piano) 224–5
— (organ) 124, 226, 228
— (timpani) 219
pedal note 212
pedal point 124–5, 147, 159
pentatonic melody/scale 242
percussion
— (instrumental category) 219
— notation 219–22
— section (of orchestra) 232–3, 235
period 175
phrase (irregular) 183–6
phrase (regular) 175–83, 185–6

Phrygian mode (see modes,
traditional)
pianoforte 223–5, 231, 235
piccolo 208, 233, 235
pitch (standard) 242
pivot (chords & notes) 141–4, 147–8,
152, 158
plagal modes (see modes, traditional)
plainsong 237–43, 250
plectrum 223
polyphony 126
polytonality 244–5
portamento 199
preparation (of suspension) 121

quartet 229–31
quintet 229, 231

rāg 241
reciting note 240
recorder 207
reed 209–12, 218, 227
resolution 118, 121, 123, 155, 161,
166
retardation 121
retrograde 249
rhythm
—, ametrical 250
—, plainsong 238
— in 20th century 250
rhythms, non-retrogradable 250–1
roll (see drum strokes)
round 128

SATB 106
saxhorn 217
saxophone 209, 212
scales
—, gapped 242
—, modal 239–41
—, pentatonic 242
—, whole-tone 245–6
score
—, full 232–5
—, miniature/pocket/study 232
—, open 108
—, piano 232
—, short 108
—, vocal 108